Also by author Terry White:
'Where the Reflecting River flows'
(A collection of poems)
Farthings Publishing 2017

The Lemon Tree

Terry White

This edition published in Great Britain 2017 by

Farthings Publishing,
8 Christine House,
1 Avenue Victoria,
Scarborough YO11 2QB

http://www.Farthings-publishing.com

ISBN 978-0- 244-76937 - 6

April 2019 (h)

DEDICATION

I would like to dedicate this book to my many friends both past and present, and in particular my mum and dad who started my path to this wonderful life.

ACKNOWLEDGEMENTS

I would like to acknowledge the help given me by Farthings Publishing of Scarborough, in getting my book into print and also to Barrie Petterson, the artist who designed and produced the cartoon for the front cover. His cartoon shows the incident related on page 162 of this book.

CONTENTS

THE LEMON TREE

As the wind of change is blowing through the mists of time I see,
That life can be bright and bitter like the fruit of the lemon tree.
Of years I am now older, as the seasons slip away.
I think of friends and places that have passed along my way.

My days of youth and childhood, I dwell on more and more.
But they are left forever like shells upon the shore.
Those years were hard but happy, filled with summer sun,
Now to secret caves and woods my thoughts so often run.

The world is always turning, as in life it always will,
And of those friends and places, are they remaining still?
Now through my children's children I once again return,
Though older, am I wiser, or am I still yet to learn?

Years become just numbers like pages in a book.
But will I find the answers by turning back to look?
Time becomes a circle filled with thoughts and memories
My past now becomes the future, for the seeds of the lemon tree.

Terry White

INTRODUCTION

I wanted to give an insight to all the changes and advancement in my life. Everything I have recalled is true, except for the names of those people involved, whose names, apart from my own family's names, I have altered to save them and their dependents, from any accidental embarrassment that might occur.

AND OF THOSE DAYS

Through a maze of tangled webs and dreams that lay unsigned.
Of rambling hills and photo stills reflected in my mind.
Where shadows dance between the clouds and laughter fills the air.
Along those once forgotten paths I will travel there.

Terry White

CHAPTER 1

WELCOME TO MY WORLD

I cannot especially recall that one defining moment in time when I became aware that I had joined this world, certainly not when I was born, and that comes as a relief, because it was on January 8th 1947 that I, Terry White first entered into this life, and into one of the bitterest English winters in living memory. I was never told of the precise time; or weight of my birth, I suppose I was just another happening, nothing special just like ordering an extra bag of coal from the coal man. I was the youngest of four children born to Edward and Catherine White. Dad had been away in foreign lands for five years fighting for King and Country, so in retrospect I suppose I was a celebration for the end of the war, although another mouth to feed at that time was nothing much to celebrate, so perhaps I was kept on the breast for as long as possible.

Mum and dad already had two daughters and a son by the time the war intervened, but after the war; I entered into the White clan. Teresa was the eldest, a year later another girl Francis was born, and then the year after Francis, Ted entered into the world. Perhaps the war was a blessing in disguise, because the way mum and dad were reproducing not only would they have run out of names, but the font at the local Catholic Church would have needed to be topped up quite regularly. There was a thirteen-year gap between Ted and myself, and very much a difference in both looks and personality, so we were not really blessed with brotherly love.

As I have already mentioned I cannot clearly remember any magical moments from my first early years, however I can piece together a few grainy memories. I can vaguely recall one day sitting on a monstrous homemade rocking horse (although it looked more like a fearsome dragon) pushing with all my might to make the large chunk of wood move. Dad had constructed the fearsome looking horse from an assortment of wood and nails, and for his piece resistance for the horse's mane, he had nailed a mop head onto its neck. (Dad had no finesse with anything; his motto to home improvements was 'why use a screw when a four-inch nail will do') At last, and to my delight the cumbersome rocking horse began to slowly rock back and forth. Suddenly an ear-piecing wail brought the horse and myself to an abrupt halt. Tabby's tail (the half-domestic tomcat: half mountain lion) had become trapped under the heavy wooden horse. Tabby, was lying flat out on his stomach on the living-room carpet uttering an ear piercing wail, while his front paws were in perpetual motion, trying in vain to drag his trapped tail from the monstrous rocking horse, while at the same time digging out huge amounts of pile with his large claws from the already thread bare carpet while I sat unmoved and bemused, looking down at Tabby's predicament. Mum, on hearing Tabby's terrifying screeching dashed in from the kitchen and scooped me up from the now stationary rocking horse. Freed at last, Tabby, with one last screech, and with strands of carpet entwined in his claws, spitting and hissing, he bolted from the living room, through the open kitchen door and into the small back yard, before scaling a six-foot boundary wall in one huge leap.

Another time I can recall, when 1 was standing happily swinging back and forth on our front wooden gate when Mrs Cowan, an elderly widow who lived in the same street, came into view. With great excitement I began to shout; "Mrs Cow, Mrs Cow."   (I had not yet learnt how to pronounce my words coherently.) However, Mrs Cowan a

God-fearing woman, with a look of anger on her face, bent down towards me and snarled.

"No! No! You horrible little boy, my name is not Mrs Cow, it is Mrs Cowan. Now what is my name?"

For a few seconds there was silence as Mrs Cowan glared down at me, obviously waiting for my correct pronunciation, however, I did not quite understand what she was saying, but with a smile on my face and bouncing up and down on the gate, I bawled out with glee.

"Moo Cow... Moo Cow... Moo Cow..."

Even now humour has always been my answer to pomp and nastiness.

Dad was born in Hull, but unfortunately at two years of age his father died of a liver disease, yet soon after his father's death his mother remarried and they all relocated to Dumple Street in Scarborough (now replaced by Auborough Street). Dad had a very hard brutal childhood with his new dad, so he was perhaps relieved when death intervened once more when at the age of eleven his step father died of cancer. Dad was a tall slim man who was very strong, and worked extremely hard from a very early age. Like most of their generation mum and dad had seen; and had been through many hard times before the war, in which dad served for five years. A dedicated family man, dad was liked, and respected by everyone who knew him. He was a hard-working honest man, with a quick sense of humour. Dad always held a belief and a hope that the so-called 'good old days' (a saying that he always detested) would never return, and in later years he recalled to me the hardships and the struggles that his generation had to endure. One particular circumstance reinforced his beliefs when a young boy in the neighbourhood was taken seriously ill. A doctor was sent for, however; because his parents could not afford the doctor's fee the boy was refused any treatment.

The neighbours though quickly rallied and held a whip round, however by the time the doctor came again the boy had died. I also recall when I was much older, dad telling me of how; during rare quiet periods of the war, young men of all trades and occupations, and from every corner of Britain, who had been recruited to fight in the war, (most of them had never been more than five miles from their home town, city or village) would gather together and discuss the appalling social conditions and the poverty that they and their families had to endure during the twenties and thirties. All of them were determined that after the war things would definitely need to change for them and their families. Dad clearly recalled with delight how, after the war, the first British General election for a number of years was held, and Winston Churchill the revered wartime Prime Minister and the leader of the Conservative party was expected to romp through the elections, but to a shocked world both he and his party were resoundingly beaten, a typical British democratic answer to a peoples' demand for fairness and justice.

I was born and spent all of my single life in James Street, a small four bed-roomed terraced house, in the North East Yorkshire coastal town of Scarborough. However, for the first few years of my life I never really knew the real names of our neighbours, not because of any ignorance or indifference on my part, but because of dad's penchant for nicknames. The neighbours on one side of our house were two elderly sisters. One was a childless widow, a huge woman with a bosom like two barrage balloons; and with a booming voice to match. The other sister was a slim timid spinster who wore thick tortoise shell glasses, and to dad's great amusement had spent all her working life on the factory floor in an iron foundry in Sheffield. Their nicknames are still etched in my mind as;

'fat en' and 'thin en.' Another neighbour a was well-spoken bespectacled retired music teacher; Mr Tetley, who gave piano lessons. Dad had christened him 'Mozart,' and although he joked a lot dad had a great respect for 'Mozart'. However, unfortunately Mr Tetley suffered from an acute problem of wind. One winter tea time dad, having arrived home from a wet, cold, hard day's work, was sitting eating his tea while Mozart was sitting talking to mum. Suddenly Mr Tetley rose up, excused himself and quickly walked to the back door, but as he closed the door behind him he broke wind very loudly. Dad quipped, "And that was Mozart's 5th symphony in G minor".

Across the road was 'Gentleman Jim', and as his name suggested, he was always immaculately dressed in a smart suit, highly polished shoes, a crisp white shirt and a tie, and with greased down hair. He, believe it or not, was an office clerk at the local slaughterhouse. His wife 'Flirty Gertie' was a dyed blonde haired, overdressed woman, who wore huge rings on her fingers and flirted with any male that she came in contact with. Smiling at herself and patting her hair, she constantly admired her reflection in the shop windows. They only had one son, who at that time would be in his late teens; he was thin and pale looking, and very effeminate, and worked as a window dresser in a local department store. Today he would be cast as 'Gay'. Dad named him from a character in one of my comics, 'Pansy Potter.' Further up the street were Mr and Mrs Woodhead and their large family. When he was a small boy Mr Woodhead had fallen out of a tree while stealing apples, in the process breaking both his legs, but unfortunately, although he recovered he became extremely bow-legged. Dad always thought he looked like a cowboy missing his horse, so Mr Woodhead then became 'Tex Ritter,' at the time a popular movie cowboy, but then later dad shortened his name to 'Tex.'

Dad cleaned the house windows himself, after dismissing the regular window cleaner because as dad stated 'He only cleans the b----- middle of the window panes!' From then on the window cleaner became known as 'Porthole Jack'. Sam Harris the milkman, nearly sliced his finger off trying to open a tin of sardines. Dad howled with laughter when he was told and from then on Sam became 'Slasher Harris,' a name poor Sam took to his grave. Arnold Heppington, a childless widower, was retired, and he was always accompanied by a very old spaniel dog who just looked like him. Arnold had a very small shop in the street; repairing bicycles and dad renamed him 'Bicycle Bill'. Those were just a few of the many nicknames that dad had invented, but only within our own household were those nicknames used and understood.

All my mates liked my dad; he was always a joker. Mum always wore the same old coat, even though she had a wardrobe full of clothes, which dad kept on reminding her. One day sitting with my elder brother and sister, dad said,

"Well, if your mum won`t listen to me, I`ll make sure she won`t wear that b----old horse rug no more."

With that he took a pair of large scissors and cut off one arm of my mum's coat, then put it back on the clothes rack. We were all helpless with laughter at mum's face as she put on her coat with one arm of it missing.

Mum originated from Gateshead, and she was the eldest daughter in a family of thirteen. Mum never received much education because when she was very young she was commandeered by her parents to help with the cleaning, feeding, and generally helping her mother to look after her huge brood of offspring. So it was no wonder that mum escaped that bleak noisy environment to seek employment as a chambermaid in the more sedate coastal town of Scarborough. Mum, except for her addiction to hard work was different in every way to dad. She was small, plump, and rarely laughed. However, when I look back on her early years, what had she to laugh about? Mum also was a devout Catholic, and to dad's displeasure, (who was a firm disbeliever) the front room was treated like a shrine, adorned with religious statues and pictures of Jesus and the Virgin Mary. Although Teresa, Francis, and Ted had attended the local Catholic school, dad, and surprisingly Mum, believed that the education that they had received at St Peters Catholic school was very poor and inadequate, so at school age I attended a non-religious school, Friarage County Modern. The walls in most of the rooms of our home displayed pictures of religious scenes, which mum regularly bought from the second-hand shops. However, whenever any panes of glass of the windows of the house needed repairing dad would remove one of the pictures from the wall, and take out the glass from the frame for the broken window pane, although he would say to a very displeased mum, before he removed the picture from the wall,

"Well Kate, make up your mind which one is it to be this time, The Crucifixion, or The Last Supper?"

Every family is supposed to have a skeleton in their cupboard; well our skeletons were hiding in that cupboard for a long time. Both sets of grandparents had died before I was born. However, many years later, Teresa, my eldest sister informed me that mum's dad had been a money lender, while our dad's father was a lodging house keeper, and his wife, our Grandmother had very strong gypsy origins. Now, whenever l look at pictures of dad when he was younger and particular Ted, with their tough brown skin and black hair, the gypsy connection does seem to run strongly in the White family. Therefore, it seems that my ancestors could have come straight from a Charles Dickens novel. However, when I think of the present breed of corrupt British politicians and greedy bankers my pedigree becomes pure class.

The war had ended, and so had most of the rationing. However, in those austere post war years there were still many foods that were regarded as a luxury to most people. Although we were never flush with money, good wholesome food was an item that was never short in our home, mostly due to Mum's culinary skills. Mum, like most of her generation could make a delicious and filling meal out of the simplest of ingredients, even though there were no fancy electric gadgets, and no choice of the finest cuts of meats, and expensive ingredients; only fresh seasonal fruit and vegetables, and any sort of cheap meat or offal that she could create into a mouth-watering meal, with no snobbish rules of how food should be presented, or of what sauces to use. Yet mum would always conjure up plain and simple; but delicious food, a fact of which today's smug, so called 'Celebrity Chefs' should take note.

Every Sunday, after dinner, nobody would be allowed into the kitchen, as mum set about the weekly bake. The entire house would be filled with the mouth-watering aroma of freshly baked bread, cakes, and pies, both sweet and savoury. Monday was the weekly washday, the luxury of washing machines was to come later in life. Mum, after filling the bath in the kitchen with hot water from the copper boiler, put the dirty washing into the bath and with her bare hands she scrubbed the washing with carbolic soap, and a scrubbing brush. After emptying the bath and wringing the washing with her hands, she then put the washing through a clothes mangle in the back yard to wring out the surplus water, before hanging the clean washing on the clothes line in the back yard to dry. This was a full day's work. Supermarkets were non-existent at the time, and shop bought pastries and bread was for most people regarded as a luxury. The kitchen was always mum's domain, although sometimes dad did break through the lines and cook a meal, but as I have already stated dad possessed no finesse to anything, including cooking. Some Sunday mornings when mum had departed to early morning mass at the local Catholic Church, dad would clap his hands together and announce to my dismay that he would cook breakfast. Dad, although he considered himself to be a competent cook, would fry the items all together in a big frying pan, the revolting mess was then scooped onto the plates. One night while mum was visiting a sick neighbour, dad took it upon himself to cook pancakes for our tea. He opened a packet of dried egg powder, left over from the days of rationing, but instead of adding one tablespoon of egg powder to the flour as instructed on the tin, Dad in his humble opinion thought it needed more so he trebled the amount, the result being that the pancakes came out as thick as a cars tyre and with the same rubbery consistency and taste to match. The rule in our house regarding food was always, "No dislikes, just get it down you." And "Always leave an empty plate."

Even today after over sixty years, I can still taste that revolting sickening powdered egg.

By the time I was attending school, because of our age distance my brother and sisters had left home, so I never really had a close brother or sister relationship. Teresa at nineteen years of age had met and married Arthur, a soldier who was to serve in the Army for twenty-two years, spending the first fifteen years of their married life in Malta and Germany, although I do remember one rare, but hilarious occasion when Teresa and Arthur with their then two young children, spent their two weeks leave at our home. At the time the second floor had three bedrooms. The two very small bedrooms had no electric sockets in the rooms; however, there was one electric socket on the skirting board of the large bedroom which Teresa and her husband had occupied, so dad plugged a long electric lead into the socket and placed a wooden lamp stand onto the heavy wooden dressing table for Arthur, who was an avid reader, so that he could read his book on a night. On the first night Arthur was laid in his bed, reading his latest book, but he needed more light, so with his eyes fixed firmly on the page he was reading; he reached out for the table lamp to move it closer, but it never moved, so he gave a harder tug, Arthur was violently dragged out of his bed and with a thud he landed onto the bedroom floor. Dad, in his wisdom had screwed the base of the lamp to the top of the dressing table.

Francis, at sixteen years of age contacted TB, a deadly disease in those days, and she spent the next decade in and out of Cottingham and Beverley Sanatoriums near Hull, a three-hour bus journey from Scarborough. National Service was still in operation, so Ted, although serving as an apprentice bricklayer, volunteered to join the Parachute regiment and he was involved in the Suez Canal crisis. Later, his stint over, Ted, now a fully-fledged bricklayer spent a number of years working in London before returning back home to Scarborough. He bought a small house and a number of years later he married, so most of my childhood was spent as an only child; however, I can assure you I was never a spoilt child. Although mum had originated from a very large family, I never saw any of them, and she rarely spoke of their existence. Dad had two step sisters and a step brother but he also spoke little of them.

Although rationing had ended some years previously, certain items were still in short supply; however, there was no shortages of shops around the area, from green grocers to furniture shops, and not just in the town centre for even in the smallest terraced street you might come across a solitary butcher, ironmonger or even a barber's shop. Nearly every street had a corner shop that sold a multitude of items and stocked whatever items were available at the time. They were also the street's meeting place where opinions of the day could be aired, or the latest gossip and scandal debated. Health and hygiene laws were as yet to come, for instance, it was not unusual to ask the shopkeeper for five pounds of potatoes and half a pound of bacon, and then watch as the shopkeeper dug his hands into a large hessian sack, extract the soil crusted potatoes, weigh them, then tip them into a brown paper bag, he would then wipe his hands on his apron, before slapping a side of bacon onto a large red slicing machine; turn the large rotary handle with his right hand and with his left hand he would catch each bacon slice before placing it onto some greaseproof paper. He then weighed the slices, wrapped them up in a paper bag, then handed the two bags to the customer. The corner shop on our street had a number of dingy yellow fly papers spiralling downwards from the whitewashed ceiling, with various flying insects adhered to their sticky surface, and in the shop the distinct smell of heater paraffin which was sold by the pint, came drifting from the back room, mingled with the shop interior's pleasant odour of opened boxes of dried fruit, sacks of flour and sides of bacon, cooked ham, and a hint of marzipan, giving out a reminder of the goods for sale in the premises.

Fish and chip shops were in abundance and provided a cheap but nourishing family meal. However, the items were fried not in cooking oil, but lard, and each fish and chip shop had its own distinctive flavour. But instead of today's fish and chip shops large and varied menu, only cod, haddock, chips, and maybe mushy peas were the only choice on offer, although in some fish and chip shops fish cakes (mashed potato and fish mixed together) coated in breadcrumbs, dipped into a batter and then fried were available. Or patties, two slices of potatoes with a slice of fish between, again dipped into batter and also fried were on the price list.

Up until I was about eight years old when our financial situation began to improve mum would do all the baking herself. However, as finances increased the baker's shop would be used quite regularly. Twice a week very early in the morning, I would be sent to the back door of the baker's shop at the top of Durham Street, where all the day's baking would be in progress, to buy hotcakes. Hotcakes were large flat bread buns. Running back home with the piping hot cakes mum would slice them open, and cover them with lashings of butter, which I would devour with relish.

Besides joints of meat; the butcher's shops provided a wide variety of cooked, and uncooked items of meat., all cut to order by hand or on a giant slicing machine. Offal, besides being cheap, if cooked right could be nourishing and tasteful. Kidneys, liver, oxtail, spare ribs, tripe, and even pig's feet were popular, also the butchers baked their own pork and steak pies, or sausage rolls, in a delicious short crust pastry. Pet shops and pet food was a thing of the future, however, bones or scraps of meat for the family dog could be bought cheaply at the butchers. While at the fishmonger fish heads, and scraps of fish were given freely for the pet cat. Second hand shops were scattered widely all over the town, usually overflowing with a variety of items. Anything could be purchased, cutlery, pots, pans, crockery, ornaments, pictures and prints, bicycles, and all sorts of brit-a-backs, plus an abundance of second-hand clothes. Mum used those second-hand shops regular, although all our clothes were always purchased new.

Central heating was still in the far distant future, so gas fires, or more generally an open coal fire, provided the heating in most homes. In the winter months Mum would order two bags of coal every week from a local coal merchant. At the time we only had a small dilapidated rusty tin coalbunker in the back yard, so dad had decided to demolish the tin bunker, then he asked Ted who was now back at home, to replace it with a large brick-built coalbunker with a small opening at the bottom. Ted built the bunker alongside the back-yard wall. For a lid Dad had acquired a thick old wooden door, which he cut to size, and with the help from a friend they heaved it onto the top of the coal bunker, they then fixed two heavy steel hinges on the door lid then onto the yard wall. That same week, two black-ingrained coalmen delivered on their backs the customary weekly order. Unable to lift the lid with one hand, the two men cursing, angrily dropped their sacks of coal onto the ground and began to heave at the monstrous lid. After some grunting and cursing the men finally heaved open the huge lid. After depositing the coal into the bunker and then letting the lid shut with a loud bang, followed by some more savoury words, one of the men turned to his mate, and sarcastically commented.

"That's not a coal bunker Sid, it's a f---- bank vault."

When the winter was over and spring had arrived, dad would call in big Frank the local chimney sweep. Frank had been a sergeant in the Grenadier Guards during the war, was a tall powerfully built man. I well remember the first time I saw Big Frank; I would be about five years old. It was a bright very early spring morning; and I was drowsily squinting from my bed at the early sunlight that was penetrating through the thin cotton curtains, when I heard Frank, with his hob nailed boots, thudding and clattering, walking down the back passage. Pausing at our back gate; Frank began coughing and retching, the result from the constant breathing of the soot that had impregnated his lungs and airways. Upstairs in my bedroom under the blankets; and a little frightened, 1 listened as in between bouts of coughing and spitting Frank's deep growling voice boomed around the house. However, although still a little frightened, curiosity soon overcame me and I quietly crept down the stairs. Nervously 1 placed my hand on the living room doorknob and gently pushed open the door, and peered inside. Although Mum had covered the living room with old sheets, the feel, and acrid smell of soot was everywhere. Dad was standing next to the fireplace, a cigarette in his hand. Kneeling in front of dad was the back of a giant black figure, all his clothes were coated in thick soot. Beside the awesome figure was a bundle of wooden rods which he constantly pushed up the chimney flue, one after another, through a hole in a soot-encrusted blanket; that was covering the fireplace. Frank must have sensed my presence for he suddenly turned around and like a huge black shadow, with only the white of his eyes showing, and his white teeth gleaming against his black face, he bawled out.

"Now then lad.. !"

That sight, coupled with Frank's booming voice made me yell with fright, quickly slamming the door shut, and to the sound of dad and big Frank's bellowing laughter, I scurried back up the stairs to the safety; and sanctuary of my bedroom.

It`s strange, but a fact, that nearly every house or building in the town was painted in either a bottle green, black, or a dark muddy brown, perhaps a reminder of the previous sombre decades. Until I was about ten years old there was no inside toilet or bathroom in the house, but in the kitchen there was a cast iron enamel bath resting on splayed giant iron feet. A wooden flat table which was covered with an oil cloth was placed over the top of the bath, and Mum used this as her kitchen preparation table. However, when a bath was required the table would be removed, and hot water from the gas copper, situated in the corner of the kitchen would be carried over in buckets to fill the bath. After being used; the bath would then revert back once more to a kitchen table. The toilet was situated outside in the back yard, directly in front of the kitchen door. There were no toilet rolls just newspaper cut roughly approximately into six-inch squares, then threaded onto string and pinned onto a nail at the back of the toilet door. On a dark winter night the toilet was a very cold foreboding and frightening place to visit, especially when I was very young, and after Ted my older brother had told me that the thick furry hessian covering; wrapped around the pipes to help keep them from being frozen, were actually a giant sleeping snake, and when disturbed the snake would wrap itself around you and squeeze you to death. So it comes as no surprise when using the toilet at night I would leave the kitchen door wide open with the kitchen light burning, and dash into the toilet do my business, and dash back to the kitchen, fastening up my shorts on the way. A few years later, and much wiser, I spent many hours sat on the toilet holding a candle; while blissfully reading the Beano and Dandy comics, adrift in my own private universe.

Every day Mum and dad would rise up very early from their bed and begin their early morning chores, before

23

departing to their respective employments. However, every Sunday morning dad would look forward to his ritual lie in after his long hard manual weeks work as a builder's labourer, while mum attended the early morning mass, at St Peters Catholic Church.

One Easter Sunday; early in the morning, the sound of a band from the local Salvation Army (known to us as Sally's Gash) came marching down the street, trumpets playing, tambourines shaking, and voices singing. Suddenly they came to an abrupt halt outside our house. The music stopped and a man's pleasant gentle voice, gave out a sermon on the death and resurrection of Jesus Christ. Lying in bed, I suddenly heard mum and dad's bedroom window violently thrust open, and dad's voice call out.

"Hey! You, Colonel"

"Yes" Came the polite reply.

"Do you know; 'There is a green hill far away"?

The man replied enthusiastically.

"Why, yes we do "

To which dad said, "Good! Well go and play on it then."

Teresa, now married, was living in Malta, and Ted after doing his national service, was for the time being still living at home. Francis after two years in hospital, was recuperating at home (unfortunately two years later her T.B. was to return) so although for only a short time, (except for Teresa) we were still a family once more.

Dad liked animals, but for some unknown reason he detested cats. Francis adored any animal, but unlike dad Francis especially loved cats, and would stroke and befriend any cat that came her way. Tabby one day walked out of the house; never to return, dad unconcerned sarcastically quipped.

"He's probably joined the other cats at Chipperfield's Circus."

Francis was the only one to be upset at Tabby's disappearance, but to dad's displeasure, Francis soon adopted a replacement, a stray cat. Kitty, as Francis named her was anything but a kitten, in fact, she was a ginger female version of Tabby, but with an extremely large head that seemed to be out of proportion to the rest of her body. After much pleading from Francis and with a little coaxing from mum, dad reluctantly agreed for Kitty to stay. Although mum later had misgivings, for Kitty would hiss and snarl at anybody passing by, especially dad. They both had a mutual dislike of each other. In fact, Kitty would only allow Francis to touch and caress her. Another thing that annoyed dad was that Kitty was giving birth to kittens on a regular basis. Dad, although reluctant to do it would drown the kittens straight after birth in a bucket of water in the backyard. This may sound cruel and sadistic but in reality we could not keep them, and nobody else would take them, and unfortunately in those days there were no R.S.P.C.A. or animal welfare centre to where they could be taken for shelter, so the kittens life if abandoned, would be very short and more than likely a horrific one.

After yet another drowning, dad, pointing and scowling at Kitty, warned Francis

"The next time Ginger Lil goes too."

A few weeks later Mum was in the kitchen preparing tea, while I was playing in the living room, when dad, arrived home from work, and sat on the kitchen step to remove his heavy work boots. Suddenly he stopped, glared at Kitty's swollen stomach, and angrily exclaimed.

"She's done it again she's b------- pregnant. Right that's it".

Striding into the backyard, and ignoring mum's pleas, dad picked up a large tin bucket, and began filling it with cold water. Alarmed, but at the same time fascinated, I stood in the kitchen doorway watching. When dad approached Kitty she arched her back and hissed and snarled loudly. However, to my disappointment mum ushered me back into the living room. Though I did not witness the titanic battle outside between an outraged dad and a scratching biting Kitty, the scene was not hard to conjure up. A few minutes later an eerie silence prevailed. Intrigued, I crept once more to the kitchen doorway and peered into the back yard. At the same time Ted had just arrived back home from work and as he entered the back yard he exclaimed loudly.

"What the hell's being going on here?"

Dad, his bare arms bleeding and covered in scratches, pointed to a now silent departed Kitty, who was dripping with water and spread-eagled on the backyard floor. He growled back,

"If you're going fishing tonight Ted, on your way down drop Ginger Lill over the far pier will you."

Ted cursing dad, gently gathered up Kitty and placed the poor bedraggled cat into an old sack before Francis could witness Kitty's sorry state. As dad began to wash his scratched and bloodied arms in the kitchen sink, with now an apologetic voice, he turned towards an angry Ted and exclaimed.

"Well! Anyway Ginger Lill never did like me!"

Ted looking aghast at dad, hit back.

"Well can you b------ blame her, that she didn't like you, you kept drowning her young uns?"

Mum was very superstitious, in fact many of her sayings even now after all these years I have not come across. Thunder and lightning absolutely terrified mum, so whenever there was a storm, (although not when dad was at home) any cutlery was rapidly removed from the table, and all electric plugs in the house removed from their sockets. She would then open wide the back and front doors, regardless of the weather, her reason being;

"If a bolt of lightning struck the house it would now go straight through, and cause no damage."

However, for me, sitting and shivering, it was not very pleasant as the house became a giant wind tunnel. A speck of soot resting on the fire grate meant a stranger bearing bad news was imminent. Any person with a thick neck, according to Mum would have a short life, if salt was spilt, mum would say a prayer to herself, if not illness was sure to come to our house. If someone yawned, Mum would angrily order the person to cover their mouth with their hand, or evil spirits would enter the body. At any blasphemous words (which dad used a lot) Mum would cross herself. One day dad, angrily uttered a string of curses after trapping his finger in a cupboard door. Mum as usual crossed herself several times. Dad glared angrily at Mum and retorted.

"If you keep crossing yourself much longer Kate, your b----- head will drop off."

As I have already stated Grandma White had gypsy origins and although she died before I was born, I was given a graphic description of dad's mother many years later by the rest of the family. Grandma White lived a few streets away from us, she was a very big woman with dark leathery skin; and coal black hair and eyes, and like all widows of her age she was always dressed in black. Grandma White was admired by all the female neighbours for her fortune telling skills either with the palms of their hands, or in tea leaves. Dad had no time for superstitions, or Gypsies, and banned Grandma from doing any palm reading, or tea leaves reading while in our house, much to mum's disappointment, which was surprising because mum held a real fear of Gypsies. At the time gypsy women with large wicker baskets full of heather, or wooden clothes pegs, visited the streets, and would knock on the front doors pleading for a small payment for bunches of 'lucky heather', or clothes pegs. Mum, again to dad's annoyance always bought something even though she was inundated with clothes pegs and heather, her reason being:

"It would bring bad luck if we bought nothing from them."

One evening there was a loud knock on the door. Dad, engrossed with his evening newspaper put the paper to the floor, and strode to answer the door. A few seconds later he returned without saying a word.

Mum wiping her hands with a tea towel, as she came in from the kitchen enquired,

"Who was that knocking on the door Eddie"?

"Gypsies, b----- scrounging as usual."

Was Dad's angry response, before settling down once more to read his newspaper.

Mum wailed,

"Oh Eddie, didn't you buy something?"

Dad replied

"Like hell I did."

"Oh no, they'll put a curse on us now Eddie. "

Mum wailed once more, while crossing herself protectively at the same time. Dad, was unconcerned as he continued to read his newspaper, but he remarked.

"Oh don`t worry Kate, I`ve put a curse on her first"

Mum asked suspiciously.

"What do you mean you put a curse on her?

"I told her to f........ off".

Mum also used her own language, it sounded gibberish, but strangely we understood what she was saying. A typical example being:

"I saw what's her name from number 10 this morning, and she said she that she had bought one of those thingy bobs last week, but the what you call it has come off, so Mr who is it, from Number 46 is going to fix it when he gets home from what yer call em."

Dad possessed a dry and quick sense of humour, but he never intended to be hurtful. However, dad detested gossip, especially if it was malicious. One warm sultry summer evening mum was sat on a chair, drinking a cup of tea in our front yard, while Dad was busily engaged painting the bay window, when the nasty Mrs Heppels, the local gossip, who seemed to detest everybody and everything, stopped, and began a conversation with mum.

"Yes, Mrs White, there she was all dressed up to the hilt, with rings on nearly every finger, flashing her gaudy new coat, with her nose stuck in the air, and with that dreadful poodle of hers, trotting in front of her. Huh, even the poodle was wearing a red collar, and attached to a red lead."

Mrs Heppels then paused for a few seconds, before adding with a sneering look on her face.

"Mind you Mrs White, they do say that owners begin to look like their pets, don't they"?

Dad, without turning around, shouted out.

"And how's that monkey of yours doing Mrs Hepples."

The family doctor was revered as a godlike figure, and only in an extreme emergency was a visit to his medical kingdom deemed necessary. So, for any ailments or conditions; that mum or dad diagnosed as minor, an array of home cures was always available.

In the winter months a slight cough was a sign of an impending cold, and that was enough to send mum into the pantry, to retrieve the bowl of fat that she had saved from the Christmas goose. My protests fell on death ears, as mum ordered me to remove my shirt, and she would diligently rub a handful of the goose fat into my chest and throat, creating a warm pleasant sensation. However, the sickening aroma of the goose fat surrounded me wherever I went, and was intensified in the warmth of the classroom, alienating me not just from my fellow classmates, but also to the wrath of the teachers, so it might not come as a surprise that I rarely coughed when I was a small boy.

To make sure I was going 'regular', mum's elixir from the gods, 'California Syrup of Figs' was the answer. A bottle of black liquid that had the look of liquid tar, and the taste to go with it. Needless to say my answer was an affirmative 'yes', if I was asked, "Are you going regular?"

Not all of Mum's cures were unpleasant though. Liquorice was known as a cure for stomach upsets, and I soon found out that if I complained enough about my poorly stomach, to my delight, mum would purchase some of the twig like liquorice sticks from the corner shop however mum soon grew wise to my pretence, and liquorice was removed from her list of remedies. Dad was extremely fit, and in generally good health except for the winter months when his regular bouts of lumbago erupted, but dad also had his own favourite cure for that, 'Ralgex', a strong medical smelling stick ointment that was administered to the pain from a tube. The ointment brought relief to dad, who seemed over the years to be immune to the searing heat of the Ralgex. It was stated on the tube to 'only administer the ointment sparingly', and not to 'rub it in', however dad great faith in the Ralgex, so kneeling in front of the open fire, and on dad's instructions, mum would rub the Ralgex deep into his lower bare back. One night just before bedtime, I complained of a swollen and painful neck, which dad quickly diagnosed as muscle cramp, so with relish, he roughly massage into my neck some of his beloved Ralgex. A little while later, asleep in bed, I suddenly awoke with a deep searing burning sensation all around my neck, screaming with pain I rushed downstairs to the kitchen sink and began franticly pouring cold water all over my neck, but the water only intensified the burning sensation. Later that afternoon the burning had ceased, but my neck was bright red, and even more swollen. That same evening mum accompanied me to the doctor's surgery. The doctor, a bespectacled, kindly man, gently examined my swollen red neck, while slowly shaking his head in a shocked silence, as mum described my symptoms, and dad's treatment of 'muscle cramp'. After mum had finished speaking, and trying hard to control his anger, the doctor now seated and looking over his spectacles, leaned across his desk and replied,

"Mrs White, Terry has mumps, so what on earth possessed your husband to apply a totally unsuited and unprescribed ointment, onto a most sensitive area of Terry's body. You do realise that it could have scarred the poor boy for life?"

Shaking his head once more, and with a look of total disbelief on his face, the doctor wrote out my prescription, while he softly muttered.

"Barbaric, just plain barbaric."

Today 'community spirit' is a phrase that is used unconvincingly, but in those austerity times that spirit really did exist. Nobody was better than anybody else, and nobody tried to be better than anyone else, if someone was lonely or in need of assistance, especially the elderly, help was only just a doorstep away. Children roamed the streets and surrounding areas free and safely, but with the added knowledge that any wrong doings, which brought complaints to your door, would be dealt with swiftly. It may seem that mum, and especially dad, were strict disciplinarians but rules were made, and were expected to be obeyed. My sense of humour, fun, and hard work was inherited from my dad. Dad made and repaired most things, and time permitted he was a well-read reader of books, he also possessed a healthy knowledge of most worldly events. However, dad first and foremost was a practical man. Dad cut hair, mended shoes, decorated, and could do most D.I.Y. jobs around the house. But although he was always busy, dad still found the time to play the mouth organ and the spoons, he could sing, and he tapped danced extremely well. Dad possessed a quick and wicked sense of humour but he was never vindictive. Mum excelled at cooking and cleaning, and she always seemed to be working, if not at home, then at various other employments, yet mum made sure that food and clean clothes for the family were always at hand. Although money was tight no debts were owed, and both mum and dad were held in high regard by everybody. Although these were not words that were bounded about at the time, I now realise that

'I loved mum and dad.'

CHAPTER 2

GAMES, GANGS AND ADVENTURES

I suppose on reflection, my early days seemed idyllic and carefree compared to the previous generation's childhood, which on reflection they were, however, although the war had ended over a decade ago and rationing had ceased, for the majority of the people the mid-fifties were still austere. After the war, it was a slow process returning to some kind of normality, and a few items were still in short supply, but there was a genuine feeling of change in the air. To the envy of the world Britain had established the National Health Service, bringing a promise for a better and fair treatment of life for all, and many of the once dreaded diseases like scarlet fever, rickets, and T.B. were now being eradicated. In the media, television was still in its infancy so radio ruled supreme with the news and entertainment. A sure sign that change was definitely in the air was the explosion of rock and roll, which brought a new word to the world, 'Teenagers' but I was not yet old enough to understand the music or the changes happening to the country. Although the majority of the population was still struggling we all shared in the same circumstances. Nobody really felt neglected or deprived; especially children, any game or pastime where money was required could be substituted by lively and inventive fertile minds. Even though I had many friends, I spent most of my time with just five. I suppose we could be termed a gang, but in reality, we were just four boys who enjoyed doing things together all the time. Dave Wilson lived a few streets away from me, and we spent a lot of time together. Dave was my best mate, and we were always on the lookout for something different to do, especially if it meant a certain amount of risk or devilment was involved. We also possessed the same kind of humour and we could both see the funny side of any situation. The other three boys also lived around our area.

Eric Barstow was a red-faced heavyset lad whose dad owned a butcher's shop. Eric was more prosperous than the rest of us, because he was the only one whose parents owned their own premises, the butcher's shop, and the large house next door, so compared to the rest of us Eric and his family were rich. However, Eric always regarded the rest of us as equals and he would share everything with us, and he possessed a cheerful and happy nature, unlike Pete Harrison.

Pete had mood swings, was not very adventurous and he seemed to see the down side of any situation. Perhaps his insecurity stemmed from the fact that he was an only child and that his dad had abandoned Pete and his mother when Pete was just a baby, (we never did find the reason why). In addition, Pete's mother was over protective, she regarded the rest of us as mischievous troublemakers, and she tried unsuccessfully to steer Pete away from our company. Sam Dawson was on the edge of our gang, and if you happen to stand near him, you would understand the reason. Sam came from a large impoverished family. His dad was a sadistic bully who never worked, and he seldom rose out of bed until mid-morning. Sam's dad had never held down a regular job, relying mostly on handouts or odd jobs down on the fish pier or any other menial jobs in the bottom end of town that might gain him some money for his cigarettes and beer, because the pub was where he spent most of his time and money. Sam's mother was a pitiful woman, who looked old well before her time; she was very thin and bedraggled, with a haunted look on her face.

When I think back it is a miracle that Sam and the rest of his family survived the terrible conditions that they had to endure. Sam unfortunately was the youngest of the Dawson clan, I say unfortunately because that put Sam firmly at the bottom of the pecking order of his two sisters and three brothers. Sam had a permanent runny nose and he wore national health glasses but with one lens missing, (the lens kept dropping out so Sam kept the lens in his trouser pocket all the time.) Sam wore hand me down clothes, and even wore his elder sister's cardigans and jumpers. The other boys and girls in the neighbourhood teased Sam relentlessly, and although he possessed no real friends, Sam was always obliging and eager to please. Though we also teased him, we genuinely felt sorry for Sam and allowed him to tag along with us. Except for Eric, toys, board games, and books were practically non-existent to the rest of us. However, established street games like hide and seek, marbles, football and cricket were always popular, but the games and adventures we enjoyed the most were those that we played out spontaneously. After the war Scarborough Council had set upon an agenda to build new council estates on the outskirts of the town, and in the process they began to demolish all the old dilapidated houses and deserted buildings in and around the town centre. Behind our street, James Street, a number of old buildings, small terraced streets, and alleys were demolished and the area flattened; and it was designated to be a coach park for the summer weekend 'Day-Trippers'. But during the week and in the winter months it became a car park for all kinds of lorries and work vans. The area was William Street Coach Park, but we called it 'the buildings.' Except for the summer weekends, the buildings became one huge playground for both the boys and girls. Football, cricket, hopscotch, skipping, and numerous other games were always on the go on the coach park. The buildings also became a fly tipping ground for the local community, so it was not unusual to find that overnight someone had deposited any unwanted piece of furniture or household items ranging from old armchairs, gas cookers, pans, and various other old and broken things. Until the council removed the unwanted rubbish, they could provide a pleasant deviation from our usual games. I once recall us having great fun with a discarded false leg and strap. Each of us took turns to kick a ball with it, or took the leg for a walk.

Alternatively, causing havoc by chasing and frightening the girls around the buildings with the false leg in our hands. However, there is only so much fun that you can have with a false leg. Therefore, as a finale we pushed the false leg through a pair of discarded trousers, filled the other leg with rags, tied an old pair of boots onto the bottom of the trousers, then placed the pair of trousers mid-way under an abandoned car, with just the bottom half of the trousers' showing. Shouting with alarm and concern, we ran up to two council workers who were loading rubbish onto a truck nearby, and began frantically pointing at the car.

"Mister, mister, there's a dead body under that old car."

The men at first ignored us, but concerned at our alarm, they walked slowly over to where we were pointing. The two workers paused and stared in horror at the realistic looking trousered legs that were sticking out from beneath the car. However, after bending down to examine the suspected corpse they soon realised that they had been duped, and uttered a stream of foul-mouthed curses, while shaking their fists in our direction, while we, from a distance cajoled and laughed at them unashamedly.

In the winter months when it had been snowing, the buildings became our very own Antarctica. Waging snow ball fights, making slide runs, rolling huge snow balls around the coach park, and, if it was still snowing, all the better. How many times when a snowstorm mercilessly whipped across the buildings, with snow clinging on to our clothes, had we enacted the perilous journey of Captain Scot, as he and his brave men, hands on each other's shoulders, walking in a single file enduring the cruel Arctic blizzards in our brave attempt to discover the South Pole. Only to be brought back to normality with Pete whining that his feet were freezing and we could all wind up in hospital with pneumonia, or Sam, trying unsuccessfully to clean the snowflakes off his single lens spectacles, while wiping the two frozen streams from his nose with the back of his hand. When the snow was thick and prolonged the 'Noggy Banks' which overlooks the Marine Drive were transformed into a white winter wonderland. Of the many games that we played on the snow-covered banks, tobogganing was the ultimate sport. However, only Eric had a shop bought skeleton toboggan, and although we all took turns using the toboggan, I desperately wanted one of my own, so I turned to my ever-resourceful dad. Dad of course built his own creation, consisting of a flat piece of wood nailed onto two thick pieces of wood; nailed across the bottom of the wood that formed the sides, with a long length of string intended to pull the heavy contraption. Dad nailed on to the bottom of the sides two strips of thin shiny metal acquired from 'Swifts' a local metal factory's scrap yard. Although, to my delight the toboggan was easily the faster of the two toboggans going down the banks, it required two of us to heave the toboggan back up the banks. One night, Dave zoomed down the banks on my toboggan and tumbled off, but the toboggan carried on at great speed for a few metres, before colliding into a large boulder and promptly disintegrated. All of us gathered around the heap of broken wood just staring at it for a few moments until Pete asked.

"What are you going to tell your dad Terr?"

Still in a daze of disappointment, I dolefully replied.

"Aw. I don't know. I suppose I'll just say somebody stole it."

We all laughed when Dave quipped.

"Stole it? What, for firewood?"

One summer the council was demolishing all the old and dilapidated houses and buildings of some other streets near ourselves, and moving the tenants into the new council estates now erected on the edges of the town. During the day, we would watch in fascination as the council workers demolished the condemned buildings, with heavy hammers and saws. Other workers sawed the large timber into manageable pieces, while some burned the smaller pieces of wood in small bonfires. A bulldozer cleared and deposited the large timber and the rubble into the line of lorries waiting to remove it all to the rubbish tip (there were no skips in those days). However, for us the real fun started when the workers had finished for the day. Making sure that there was nobody about, especially any policemen, we would gather up small pieces of brick and throw them at the unoccupied condemned houses windows, yelling out if you broke one. Then we would search the houses looking for any unwanted items that the tenants had left behind. Brushes, shovels, tools, old bikes, wooden chests, comics, newspapers, washtubs, old furniture (shoving our hands down the back of settees and armchairs for any lost coins.) The real prizes though were any gas masks left over from the war. With delight, we would put on the gas masks and charge up to the bedrooms with copper pipes or wooden sticks, and pretend to shoot down below at the hordes of German soldiers trying to smoke us out. Alternatively, like Dan Dare and his intrepid crew, dashing from house to house trying to evade Emperor Ming's guards in the gas-filled tunnels on the planet Darruss. One day we had searched some houses but we had found nothing. We climbed up one of the houses to the attic bedrooms, shoved open a bedroom door and barged in, and then we froze. In a corner a scruffy tramp, holding a brown paper carrier bag in one hand and clutching a bottle of beer in his other hand, was snoring loudly in a corner of the room. Suddenly his bloodshot eyes shot opened, and struggling to rise up, he roared "B----Kids, I'll strangle the f-----lot of yer." We all screamed as this wild looking man came staggering towards us, and in the rush to get out we all jammed in the open doorway. We barged downstairs but the tramp staggered after us, so we ran down the hallway to the back door. However, try as we may the door had jammed. Stilling screaming we ran back down the passage to the front door, and rushed past the tramp, who quickly made a grab for Pete by his coat collar. As the tramp glared at him, with his wild eyes, Pete cried out loudly.

"LET ME GO, LET ME GO. MUM, MUM, I WANT ME MUM."

Luckily, the back door was wide open so we dashed into the back yard then into the open alleyway, overtaken by the still petrified Pete. Ever after that incident whenever Pete moaned or complained, Dave and

I would look at each other and Yell. "I WANT ME MUM, I WANT ME MUM."

Times were still frugal, and pocket money rarely given, so a great deal of thought and concentration was required if you had any money. Comics such as the Beano, Dandy, The Eagle, or Hotspur, were always a firm reading favourite, but you could acquire them free, if you asked for them, from any fish and chip shop's supplies of old newspapers and journals. Toys, even the cheapest, were only obtainable at Christmas, so for the rest of the year they were as rare as moon dust. However, the favourite shop for a young person who clutched a three-penny, or sixpenny piece in their hand, was, without doubt the sweet shop. Most sweet shops displayed boxes of chocolates in a variety of brand names on the top shelves, while on the lower shelves, open boxes contained tempting items such as Kit Kat bars, Mars Bars, Bounty Bars. However, these items did not last for long, and besides, chocolate bars were for Christmas, and then usually in selection boxes. However, on the lower shelves, or displayed on the open counter in large jars or boxes; were far cheaper sweets. Yorkshire Mix was an assortment of boiled sweets which could be bought cheaply in one or two ounce bags, the same as Midget Gems (tiny wine gums), chewing nuts (small toffee balls coated in coco powder), or Pontefract cakes, (small soft discs made of liquorice). Sherbet, sometimes called kalie, was displayed in two large jars, one raspberry flavour, and one lemon flavour. Again, these could be bought in small paper bags, or if preferred a mix of one ounce of each colour in the same bag. The Kalie was both sour and sweet at the same time, and it stained our tongue and lips. Black jacks were small squares of soft chewy liquorice costing four for one penny, the same as fruit salads, (small fruity squares of soft toffee.) Tubes of chewing tobacco were actually long shreds of coconut covered in a coating of coco powder. Flying saucers were round edible rice paper filled with sherbet that melted as soon as you put them in your mouth. Liquorice sticks were the roots of the liquorice plant that looked like small twigs, and after sucking out all the juice, they tasted like small twigs. However, always a favourite purchase with the boys were the square packs of chewing gum with a coloured picture card inside depicting a famous footballer of the day in action. At the back of the card, it carried the footballer's details. These cards could be collected to complete a set of about twenty cards, and if you already had the footballer, bartering or swapping with the other boys became a serious business. A typical swap could be 'I'll swap you two Billy Wrights for one Tom Finney' because all the boys tried desperately to complete a full set.

The 'Bottom End' seemed to be a village within the town, a community all of its own. Most of the bottom end residents were in some way usually connected to the fishing industry, and as such, most of the businesses and shops directed their interests to the fishing community. The Ice House just behind Foreshore Road had the sole purpose of producing ice for the keelboats and cobbles, which kept the newly caught fish fresh at sea; until they reached the fish pier. On the day before they were to go out to sea, the fishermen would collect the ice in large open barrows and then transport them to their fishing craft berthed in the harbour, ready for the nights fishing. The large steam trawlers had outlived their purpose, so now just two types of fishing boats made up the large Scarborough fishing fleet. The coble was something akin to a large rowing boat but equipped with an engine, usually manned by one or two fishermen, the cobles fished through the night for not just the fish but crabs and lobsters, that lived in the local bays and coastline. The keelboat was in-between a trawler and a coble, with a covered cabin and cramped living quarters, which could accommodate about four men, and they fished further a-field for most of the week, for a variety of larger fish. There were bakers, butchers, fish and chip shops, and other small corner shops in the bottom end However, in abundance were the public houses, each with their own clientele. The gigantic stone built covered Market with its assortment of small stalls, seemed to be the gateway to the bottom end, but you had to climb up some steep steps to reach the huge hall. The basement, were once used as a cattle market and abattoir. Above, on the huge market floor all sorts of veg, herbs, fruit, and meat were sold. 'Kays book stall' sold not just second-hand books but also second hand comics and scraps (coloured sheets of paper images that would be cut out and pasted in a 'scrap book'). Outside the market, 'Wells' was an old wooden shack that sold newspapers and magazines, Maurice Wells the owner's son was a well-loved character who delivered not just the daily papers but also the nightly local paper. Only about thirty yards from the Market was the Friarage Infant, Junior, and senior schools that I attended. Situated just below the remains of the Scarborough Castle was the Graham Sea Training School, which as the name suggests was for boys from the age of eleven whose career were designated to be on the sea. Opposite the market in Leading Post Street was a lodging house used by tramps and other destitute men known locally as the 'Three Penny Bedders.' The price for a bed for the night was just three old pennies. Dad informed me that sometime before the war a thick rope fixed approximately four feet from the floor; and to the sides of a large room, and for the price of one penny, the unfortunate men could lean over the rope to sleep. We were all attending Friarage junior school so we mixed with a number of 'bottom enders', who were friendly and we became good friends with most of them. Many fun filled hours we spent playing, and discovering things around those streets and buildings of the bottom end, especially the harbour and all its surroundings.

Swimming was something we had all learned at an early age, not just, for our own safety, but living in a seaside resort meant that swimming was one of the very few pastimes that required little money. We all could swim but Dave and I loved swimming. Scarborough has two bays, 'The North Bay' and 'The South bay.' In the summer month's lifeguards wearing yellow jerseys; would patrol up and down in a single engine boat, approximately six metres from the shore, warning any swimmers who might have strayed too far from the beach to return to safety. Dave and I would swim out to the patrolling lifeguard's limit, and keeping about 10 metres apart we would wait patiently until the lifeguard approached, and then one of us would swim further out to sea. The lifeguard would motor over to him and order him back to the shore. In the meantime, the other boy had begun to swim further out to sea. The lifeguard suddenly seeing the other boy motored franticly to him and gave him the same command. The first boy then turned around from shore and once more swam back out to sea. The furious lifeguard roared back towards him; yelling hysterically again for him to return to the shore. Dave and I would repeat this pattern a number of times until the poor lifeguard would be weary and seething with anger. Together Dave and I would then swim back to the beach to join the other lads, who were jeering and laughing at the frustrated lifeguard. Although our little bit of fun soon ended abruptly one very sunny afternoon. After baiting the frustrated lifeguard, Dave and I laughing as usual, waded back to the shore, only to find that the other lads had mysteriously disappeared. Puzzled, Dave and I, with hands over our foreheads to mask the blazing sun, scanned the crowded beach wondering where our mates had gone, when suddenly a hard slap at the back of both of our heads sent us reeling down onto the beach. Our ears ringing, we squinted up to see another yellow jersey lifeguard glaring down on us. With a sneer on his weathered beaten face, the lifeguard bellowed,

"Now, how's that for a laugh you little buggers, the next time you pull a stunt like that I'll kick your arses up and down the b----- beach"

The North Bay had a glorious large outdoor swimming pool, which was only open in the summer months. The pool had three diving boards and a slide, and situated only a short distance from the beach. The swimming pool was very popular with both the locals and visitors alike. Unfortunately, for us there was the task of finding the money for the one shilling (five pence) admission fee. Although the other boys liked swimming it was Dave and I (if we could raise the money) who would spend as much time as possible at the pool. If it was raining all the better because to our great amusement, as soon as it started to rain there would be a mad scramble by the holidaymakers to evacuate the pool, leaving just a small minority of us to enjoy the space and freedom of the near deserted pool.

Sam possessed no swimming trunks at all, while Eric owned a pair of smart black nylon trunks. However, Pete, Dave and I wore the standard cheap woollen swimming trunks. The first time Sam did actually have the money, and visited the swimming pool was unforgettable. As we all undressed in the boys changing room, Sam opened up his torn bedraggled piece of towel to reveal a large khaki pair of tattered shorts belonging to one of his elder brothers. We laughed as Sam began putting them on as the shorts were far too big for him. So Sam had tied a piece of orange fishing line around his thin waist to keep the shorts in place Once outside the dressing room and into the blazing sun, a pale and undernourished, squinting, Sam made a sorry sight, so much so that the swimming pool superintendent came charging up to Sam and bellowed.

"You can`t go in the pool like that you scruffy little b----- you`ll frighten the visitors to b---- death, you look like a refugee from Belson. Now get out of here"

Wearing those woollen trunks when in the water was a nightmare, as it felt as though you were wearing a grotesque oversized nappy, but even more frustrating was the fact that the trunks, when wet, increased in both weight and volume. When finally you did succeed in heaving yourself out of the water, the back of the trunks hung nearly down to the back of your knees like a net full of fish, while huge amounts of water cascaded down your legs. Dave and I would look in envy at the bright coloured stylish nylon or rayon trunks of the more prosperous boys, and we vowed that one day we too would acquire a pair of those swimming trunks. The following year, after having saved some money, both Dave and I became the proud owners of a pair of light blue rayon swimming trunks. Putting on those trunks in the dressing room, and then proudly walking around the pool edge like two posturing film stars is a memory that still lingers with me to this day.

Unless we were going to the swimming pool, we never took our swimming trunks or a towel with us. In the summer months, our standard dress would be just a tee shirt, shorts, and plimsolls, and if we did decide to play in the sea or a river, we would just simply remove our tee shirts and plimsolls. Of the two bays, the South Bay was by unanimous consent our favourite bay for it was the nearest to the fishing harbour, and the hustle and bustle of the beach and promenades. When the tide was low, we spent many happy hours exploring the dozens of rock pools below Scarborough Spa, moving the heavy rocks to see what mysterious creatures might be lurking beneath. One day we came across a very unusual looking fish stranded in a rock pool. Although we were familiar with all the local sea life, this fish intrigued us. I attempted to catch the fish with my hands, but cried out in agony when one of my hands touched its spiny fin. For the rest of the day I was in agony with a mild form of blood poison. From that day on, we treated the weaver fish with a great deal of respect.

At the far end of the more sedate North Bay is Scalby Beck, that consists in a number of small streams that merge into one large stream and eventually flows into the North Bay. If we planned to visit the 'Beck' our Mums would provide a few sandwiches for the day, because it was definitely a full days outing. The beck flowed for about two miles into the estuary of the North Bay, passing through a deep gorge with trees and shrubs on both banks. Apart from the usual swimming, and water games, we played many other games in the beck and surrounding woods and scrublands. A popular but dangerous attraction was the 'Pipe Bridge' a large metal sewer pipe that ran approximately ten metres above the beck from bank to bank; across a very narrow metal bridge, with spiked railings at both ends, but those were no deterrent to us. For a dare, each one of us would, after wriggling around the railings, straddle the iron pipe, and slowly slide our way along the pipe to the other side. While down below the other boys would throw small pebbles or shoot them from our home-made wooden catapults at the person attempting the crossing. As I write now, I am amazed, even though we all must have slid across the pipe bridge, and endured the barrage many times, that there had been no serious incidents. By about midday we would be ravenous, so finding a suitable flat patch of land near the beck; we would stretch out on the grass, eager to eat our sandwiches, except for Sam, who nonchalantly began throwing stones into the water professing he wasn't really hungry, yet enviously looking back at us through his one lens spectacles. Sam was hypnotised at the sight of our little bundles of potted meat, and jam sandwiches. Grinning at each other, we would roll our eyes, and make rapturous noises as we ate our sandwiches tormenting a very hungry Sam, however, we would always save a sandwich each for Sam, saying.

"Here you are snotty, get these down yer."

Sam grinning, but saying nothing, eagerly snatched the sandwiches from our hands, and devoured them in seconds. Though we teased him mercilessly, there was a genuine fondness and protectiveness from the rest of us towards Sam, which an incident one sunny afternoon at the beck confirmed. Revitalised after having eaten our sandwiches, we dug a large hole in the ground and then filled it with water before creating a colony of frogs picked up from the Beck and placed them into the hole. Suddenly from the surrounding bushes a gang of three older lads appeared. Straight away, looking at their scowling faces, we suspected trouble. Whooping with sadistic delight the older boys ran past us and destroyed our pool, and then began to stamp on our colony of frogs. We were all animal lovers and protested loudly, none more so than Sam, who crying, fell down onto his knees, and with his arms spread protectively across the hole, pleading for them to stop the mass slaughter. The youths sneered and jeered at Sam, while the tallest and nasty of them pulled Sam up by his arm and snarled.

"You snivelling scruffy little b-------, fancy crying over some f----- slimy frogs."

"Leave him alone, he's done nowt to you!" Eric protested loudly.

Looking back towards his mates, the lad jeered.

"Hey, Did you hear that lads, fatso said to leave the rag bag alone, so, what do you say?"

One of the other youths replied.

"I know Steve, stick the scruffy, four eyed rag bag's head in the hole with them then if he likes frogs that much"

Steve nodded his head in agreement

"Yea, that's a great idea Mick."

Smirking, Steve gripped Sam's arm even tighter, making Sam wince with pain.

The usually passive Eric slowly walked up to Steve and growled "I've told you once and I won't tell you again, just leave him alone!"

"O yeah, and wha—"

Before Steve could finish his sentence Eric's large fist exploded into Steve's face, propelling him onto his back. For a few seconds there was an eerie silence between both gangs, until a shocked Steve sat up from the ground, took his hand from his face, looked in horror at his bloodstained hand and whined.

"I'm bleeding, I'm bleeding, he's broken my b----- nose".

Dave, Pete, and myself, laughed, and encouraged by Eric`s stance approached the other gang fully expecting a fight. However, to our surprise Steve suddenly jumped up and ran past his mates, wailing loudly, before staggering back into the bushes, quickly followed by his shocked mates. That day I learned two things. Never judge a person's character on first instance. Eric seemed a passive unassuming lad; which he was most of the time, but every person's tolerance has a limit. Bullies of any sort who I detested, and I still do, intimidate the weak and helpless. However, as I have found over the years, bullies are cowards at heart, and unless backed up in numbers, they always submit if faced with resistance.

The ancient walls of Scarborough Castle straddles like a sleeping stone giant high above the two bays. The castle`s history dates back over many centuries of conflict and wars, and once it was unsuccessfully besieged by the army of Oliver Cromwell. However, for nearly one hundred years the castle has remained uninhabited, its grounds and ruins were acquired by The National Trust and it has become a popular tourist attraction. However, for the majority of the young 'Bottom Enders', of the time, the ruined castle's outside perimeters were a giant playground.

The old moat below the castle's walls, which ran around the south side of the castle, dried up centuries ago but its indentation remains, although now covered in thick grass. Only about four metres wide and approximately fifty metres long, the moat was a popular attraction to the younger generation. Sometimes rival gangs would line up opposite each other at the bottom of the moat goading and shouting, until one gang would suddenly charge towards the opposition. Although there was much shouting, yelling, and general grappling there were no weapons used, as each

49

gang fought until exhausted, and then came a mutual truce between the gangs. The two gangs sometimes continued their rivalry with a friendly game of football. Two goals marked out by using jumpers as goal posts, and sometimes members of one gang joining the opposition side easily sorted an uneven set of players. On one such occasion, we met a gang smaller in number, so we agreed that Sam could join the other gang to make both the sides even. However, the opposition were not over pleased with our generous choice, but after some bickering they eventually agreed, and made Sam their goalkeeper. Although Sam was willing and eager, he was useless, and conceded a number of goals in a short time, much to the anger of the rest of his teammates. Sam in his defence claimed the ball was hard for him to see, seeing as he was wearing glasses, to which one of his temporary team mates angrily yelled back.

"Well if you put your b------ lens back in the frame instead of your pocket you thick b----- Dawson, you might see the ball better."

One day, Dave curious about the lens always being in Sam's pocket, he asked Sam.

"Hey Sam, why do you always keep that lens in your pocket all the time?

Sam just nonchalantly shrugged his shoulders and replied

"Because my Dad said if I lost it he would bash me."

I added, "What`s your dad got to do with it, I thought the glasses were free, so why don't you just get the lens put back in, or get a new pair of glasses?"

Sam shrugged his shoulders again and replied nonchalantly "Well I could I suppose, but my Dad would still bash me anyway."

The Battery, midway down from the castle is a small flat area of grassland that overlooks the South Bay. In bygone days, the Battery were once lined with cannons to defend the castle and its inhabitants from any marauding enemy invasion arriving by sea, but now it is just a deserted place. However, to us it became a means of sanctuary when tired or bored. We would sit, or stretch out on the cool lush grass during the warm summer months, talking, playing, or just staring down at all the far away activity of the crowded beach and promenades below, while in the background could be seen the splendid grandeur of the Grand Hotel, and the Scarborough Spa. During the day, the fishing harbour was full and tranquil, as the Keelboats and Cobles moored close together and bobbed up and down in a patient silence, waiting for their crews, and another night of successful fishing. In the far harbour directly below the Battery, private yachts and motor boats, once in winter bondage, gingerly made their passage through the narrow harbour mouth into the open flat bay, to join the Pleasure boats and other craft sailing around the Scarborough coastline. On a many hot summer afternoon the Battery became our own personal playground, or if too hot, looking down on the hordes of holidaymakers thronging the beach and promenades like human ants.

However, the other side of the castle, which overlooks the North Bay and the long winding road of the North Marine Drive, also had its own attractions. Next to the lush green grass and twisting paths, known locally as the 'Noggy Banks' is the 'Plateau', a large grassed area, situated below the shrubs and bushes that clusters around the foot of the castle, and like the Battery on the South side, it is a vantage point that overlooks The North Bay. The Plateau was ideal for a variety of games, and sometimes used for a night of camping, that is if you were lucky to have a tent. Among the shrubs and bushes alongside the Plateau are a number of trees, and one tree in particular, the rocking horse tree, was a great attraction. Trees and thick foliage rise up steeply to the foot of the castle walls, and deep in the centre of the bushes that overlooked the Plateau was the 'Rocking Horse Tree'. The tree had a thick length of rope permanently hanging from one of its sturdy branches ending about a half of a metre up from the ground. The rope was never removed or vandalised by anybody, and was used by different gangs of boys, to swing above the ground, like Tarzan in the jungle, or marauding pirates boarding a Spanish galleon, many happy hours were spent in and around the Rocking Horse tree playing all kinds of imaginary games.

Situated just below the Plateau and overlooking, the Marine Drive is a gathering of huge rocks and boulders, one of the huge rocks is 'Hairy Bob's Cave,' and it is etched permanently into Scarborough's folk lore history. The rock has a small window, and an opening gouged out like a doorway, although a person would need to be very small indeed to fit comfortably into the rock. Nobody actually knows why or when the holes were made or indeed if there was such a character called Hairy Bob. There have been many suggestions and numerous rumours over the years, but no actually proven facts. Nevertheless, to us Hairy Bob's cave and the surrounding rocks were always a magnet, and perhaps the mystic of Hairy Bob, made the rocks an added attraction. Just before you entered, the Plateau there was a clump of trees called the 'Little Wood'.

One summer, and to our great delight, Eric's parents had bought him a tent. That same day we erected the tent in Eric's large back yard, and then the five of us scrambled inside the tent to test it out. Although a little cramped and claustrophobic inside the tent, with great delight we agreed that we should go camping, and as soon as possible. Therefore, after many discussions and arguments we finally settled the issue, that the Little Wood was an ideal place for a campsite. The next day the planning and excitement of our first overnight camping adventure took preference over everything else. After tea, we met at Eric's house, before making our way to the plateau, and pitched the tent in the Little Wood. Then we settled down to eat the sandwiches, and drink the bottles of orange squash, that our mothers had prepared for our suppers. (Sam of course shared our sandwiches and squash). We all had catapults, but I also had a 'Diana' air pistol so it was decided that for protection against any unwanted prowlers that I would sleep next to the tent opening. Once inside the tent it took a long time for everybody to settle down, the main grumble being the smell of Sam`s feet and Pete constantly breaking wind, but eventually we began to tire. I loaded the pistol with a lead pellet and compressed the barrel, before placing the pistol on my stomach, with my finger resting on the trigger, ready for any intruder that might appear in the night; and then slowly we all eventually drifted off to sleep. Suddenly I shot up and cried out loudly in pain, I had, after falling asleep unwittingly squeezed the trigger and shot the pellet into my big toe. The next few seconds were mayhem. Because of the pitch-blackness and the tight confinement of the tent, and my yelling, everybody was in turmoil. Sam, desperately searching for his glasses, poked Dave in the eye with his elbow; Dave in turn clashed heads with Eric. However, Pete had completely lost the plot, as he jumped up violently in alarm, his head ripped through the top of the flimsy nylon tent and peering up at the black sky, Pete wailed hysterically.

"MURDER, POLICE, HELP, HELP.."

A little after midnight I was knocking gently on my front door with my big toe throbbing, and in complete disarray. Dad opened the front door standing in his baggy long johns, and looking angrily at me, he growled sarcastically.

"Enjoy your few hours of camping then, did you?

However, although a little downhearted our enthusiasm for camping never wavered. Eric's mum repaired Pete's vandalism of the tent, and about a week later with more in-depth planning, we once again set up camp in the Little Wood. This time we abandoned the idea of the air pistol for protection, as we deemed that it was unreliable and too dangerous, instead we agreed that we should have a small fire burning away from the tent, made up from bits of wood and broken tree branches, surely that would deter any intruders we reasoned. Dave suggested that if we all brought some potatoes, we could bake them in the fire, Eric added that bring along some lard, sausages, and an old frying pan, and we could fry the sausages over the fire. Earlier that day Dave had poured some petrol into an empty lemonade bottle from a container stored in his dads shed, with the sole purpose of igniting the fire. After pitching the tent, we gathered a huge pile of dead wood from the nearby shrubs and trees, we then, with the aid of a little petrol, lit a small fire away from the tent. Soon the fire was burning steadily, a little while later we pushed our potatoes into the fires edge, set aside the sausages, and put some lard in the frying pan. Sitting around the fire, drinking bottles of orange squash and lemonade, laughing and joking, we looked on hungrily at the black skinned potatoes poking at them with long sticks. However, Pete with a strange look in his eye, seemed mesmerised by the fire and he began throwing more and more wood and bush onto it, then, disregarding our protests, he thrust a stick violently into the fire sending up shoals of sparks into the blackened sky. Suddenly Dave jumped up and cried out in alarm, "Oh b------ hell, the tents on fire, the tents on fire."

A small area of the tent had actually started to turn brown. We all shot up and ran around the tent in a panic, as the browned area began to spread quickly through the flimsy nylon tent.

Eric yelled hysterically.

"Quick! Somebody grab a bottle and throw some squash or lemonade over it."

Sam, with a determined look on his face stepped forward, grabbed a bottle of lemonade and poured it over the flames. There was a whoosh, and the tent suddenly disintegrated, leaving just a scorched area of grass, and a few black particles floating gently up towards the black starless sky. For a moment, there was complete silence, broken only by the sharp crackling of the roaring fire. Eric, Pete Dave and I, looked at each other's blackened faces, before turning angrily to Sam. Sam was standing motionless, staring at the scorched grass, that seconds earlier had been our tent, and clutching the lemonade bottle that contained the petrol. The sleeve of Sam`s elder sister's cardigan was badly scorched, and his face completely black including his one-lens spectacles. With a mighty roar and in unison, we chased after a petrified Sam. The next day Eric was severely reprimanded by his parents, and forced to help in the family business for the remainder of the school holidays. Dave received a smack from his dad, and an angry lecture on the danger of using petrol. Pete also received his punishment from his mother, and ordered not to associate with such troublesome hooligans again. Sam received a beating the next morning from his ill-tempered Dad, not for the previous night's folly and danger, but simply because his dad had a severe hangover. That same night, in the very early morning, after nervously knocking on my front door, I once more stood on the doorstep, in worried anticipation of dad's reaction. The door flew open, and a furious Dad looked at my blackened, sorrowful face, and then with a smile slowly appearing on his face he asked.

"What happened this time then, an Apache war party?"

Owning a new bike then was akin to today's desire for boys to having the latest mobile phone. However, for some boys a new, or second-hand bike was not within theirs, or should I say their parents grasp. Nevertheless, for the majority of boys it was no bike at all, which included us, except for Eric of course, who owned not just any bike, but a bike with racing bar handles, and three speed gears. Yet Eric did not boast of his acquirement, and he willingly let us all have turns to ride his bike, but we all envied him so much that it spurred us to own our own bikes. A bike could be constructed together from spare parts, by visiting the local scrap yards, or refuse tip. We managed to get discarded bikes, and then by replacing any missing items we constructed something that resulted in a reasonable bike, and that gave us a tremendous feeling of achievement. Visiting the local paint shops or stores, we asked if they had any unwanted old tins of paint and brushes, after listening to our explanations they were pleased to oblige, we then painted the bikes to our own desired colours. With great pride, I had constructed not only my own bike, but also one with a fixed wheel, which meant that the pedals would only stop turning when the back wheel stopped moving. One fateful day while we all were whooping and laughing while speeding down 'Penny Back Lane 'a very steep hill, I momentary lifted both my feet off the pedals and raised them into the air. However, as I returned my feet back onto the pedals, the pedals hit my legs violently, and abruptly stopped the bike, which in turn resulted in catapulting me over the handlebars onto the road face down. My bike broken, like my pride, and with my face scrubbed and bleeding, I dolefully staggered home with my wreckage fully expecting laughter from my dad. However, I was surprised when dad not only tried to console me, but sympathised with me as well. The following week I was astounded when one night, dad came home with a lovely bike that had three speed gears and dynamo lights, which he had bought from a second-hand shop. That bike took me through many escapades and adventures, through terrains, and all kinds of weathers for four years, and even helped me on my first official part time job as a newspaper delivery boy; I only disposed of the bike when I left school to begin my apprenticeship.

CHAPTER 3

GISSA JOB

There was no such thing as pocket money when I was a boy. It was not until I left school at the age of fifteen when I began my apprenticeship, that I began to have a regular income of my own. At the time it was against the law to officially employ anybody under the age of thirteen, so until we could get an official part time job like delivering newspapers, or as an errand boy, no money was available. Even mundane things of today such as crisps or sweets were regarded a luxury, so to acquire those little luxuries a great deal of hard work; or in some cases a little cunning was needed. Scarborough was in those days, not only a very popular seaside resort but also a thriving fishing port, so there were always some ways to make a little money, especially in the summer season.

The Scarborough railway station every Saturday morning was a hive of activity in the summer months, as the incoming trains brought their crowded carriages of happy visitors arriving for a week, or two weeks holiday. From all over Yorkshire, the North East, and Scotland, because in those days very few people travelled by car, or even owned one.

So apart from those holidaymakers lucky enough to have booked their stay in one of the guest houses situated near the railway station, most had to walk while heaving their heavy suitcases and luggage. But if they could afford the fare, they could hire a taxi to get them to their holiday accommodation. However, there was another far cheaper option, select one of the many boys who were eager to transport your suitcases to your intended stay,

There were boys with handcarts, barrows, even prams, and some like us, who had constructed their own flat back trolley made of wood and covered with a blanket, and using pram wheels for transportation. We would walk up and down the long queue that were waiting for a taxi outside the railway station, shouting.

"CARRY YOUR BAGS ANYONE? "

But all the while making sure we kept well away from the long line of taxis drivers who were waiting to ferrying the visitors to their destinations, for apart from the strong language and threats, a smack on the ear was something to avoid. We were never swamped with offers, but you could usually get a fare. The first question usually asked was; 'How much?'

The standard reply was.

"Half a Crown (twelve and a half pence) Mr, (or Mrs,) any distance."

However, the journey could be from only a few hundred yards, to a mile or more, depending on the holidaymaker's actual destination, and Scarborough has some very steep hills

There were five members in our gang and between us we had constructed two trolleys. Each trolley needed two boys to manage and manoeuvre. Five is an odd number so unfortunately somebody would have to be disappointed, and that unfortunately meant Sam. This might seem unfair, but with his runny nose and his national health glasses, with one of the lenses missing, and his rag bag assortment of clothes, we all deemed that Sam was definitely an embarrassment and a put off to our Saturday enterprise. We were never greedy, maybe two-three trips each for both trolleys, and with perhaps a few shillings for tips was enough for a day's work. We always split the money four ways and of course some money was handed to Sam as compensation.

One memorable Saturday morning either because of desperation to be a full member of the gang, or to make money for himself, Sam turned up at the Railway Station with an old wooden handcart that his dad used for collecting bits of scrap metal and other sellable items. Sam had covered the gouged and splintery back of the handcart with an old ragged blanket, and although we laughed at first, to our complete surprise Sam managed to acquire a fare, an elderly couple with an equally elderly battered suitcase bound up with coarse string. By coincidence Pete Harrison and I with our loaded trolley, were following closely behind Sam and his fare, when Sam suddenly turned into a side street with a very steep hill downwards. Ignoring our shouted warnings Sam pushed his handcart on the road down the hill, with the old couple following Sam closely behind on the pavement. But they had to quicken up on their walking to keep pace with Sam. Suddenly Sam's heavy cumbersome handcart began to increase in momentum down the steep hill, with poor Sam struggling desperately trying to hold down the handles of the cart. Gathering even more speed, and without warning the cart suddenly lifted Sam completely off the ground, but Sam doggedly clung on to the handles with his legs flapping wildly in the air, while the cart continued in a straight line for a few metres more, before veering, then crashing into the opposite kerb side and in the process tippling over. This resulted in catapulting Sam over the handles and onto the ground, while throwing the battered old suitcase high up into the air. The suitcase landed back down with a huge thud onto the pavement, the string snapped and the old case sprung open throwing clothes everywhere. The sight of a sock, a vest, and a huge pair of pink bloomers dangling from a hawthorn bush growing at the side of the pavement, brought howls of laughter from passers-by, except a distressed and bruised Sam, and the angry and embarrassed elderly couple. The old man whacked Sam furiously with his walking stick. Unfortunately, the handcart was completely wrecked, resulting in Sam receiving yet another beating from his sadistic dad.

The 'Scarborough Cricket Festival' was a very popular annual event that attracted thousands of cricket lovers from all over Yorkshire. The festival was always held in September over a period of nine to ten days, and the final match was always between the current foreign touring Test Team and a select 'England Eleven' Most evenings of the festival the admission gates were thrown open for the last hour of play, and the admission was free. Sport loving pensioners and schoolboys, with little or no money relished this gesture, for it meant that they could see in action English and International cricket stars of the day competing, and completely free.

At the end of each day's play the thousands of spectators would slowly begin to make their return journeys back home, leaving behind discarded bottles, cigarette packets and all other manner of litter. All that rubbish had to be cleared and taken away before the following day`s play, and what cheaper way for the club to handle this task than to hire lots of schoolboys, to pick up the discarded rubbish. The pay was one shilling per hour (five pence in today's money) each boy was given a large hessian sack in which to put in the discarded litter, and then the boys walked in a line between the long rows of rising wooden benches around the ground, picking up the litter, supervised by the stern head grounds-man and his two assistants. Any empty lemonade bottles we would put to one-side to be returned later to the shops for the few pence deposit. Picking up the litter though was a back breaking and tedious work, so any distractions were always a welcome relief.

Dave and I had been litter picking for three nights, when on the fourth; very sunny evening, trying hard to concentrate on the boring task, a banana skin hit me at the back of my neck. Furiously looking up, and with the banana skin clinging onto my tee shirt I caught sight of Dave three rows up, laughing profusely. Annoyed and angry I picked up a discarded soggy tomato sandwich and threw it towards Dave, who, realising my intension ducked, and the tomato sandwich missed Dave, but unfortunately hit the boy behind him full in the face. Within seconds, there was mayhem among the litter pickers, with much laughter and shouting, for now everybody was throwing all manner of discarded fruit, sandwiches, and cardboard cartons at each other. The riot lasted only a few minutes though, as the grounds man mowing the playing field, jumped off his large petrol driven lawn mower, and ran across the playing field, and red faced, he jumped up and down bellowing in rage from the side of the pitch, while his two assistants trapped in the middle of the turmoil, were unsuccessfully trying to quell the raging battle. It was only through the intervention of the loud speakers situated around the ground, angrily demanding for order that the mayhem slowly subsided. A pimple faced young assistant identified Dave and I as the instigators. The fuming grounds man, without ceremony ran up the concrete steps, smacked us both around the head, grabbed both of us roughly by our shirt collars and marched us out of the cricket ground, with a angry threat to keep well away from the ground in future, thus ending Dave and I our short careers as litter pickers.

The real bonanza for earning any extra money was the six weeks of the schools' summer holidays, and the place it all happened was Scarborough's South Bay. Foreshore Road runs approximately about half a mile along the seafront. On one side of the road is the long wide beach that looks out to the open South bay. Further along the road is the old fishing harbour, the middle pier, and the far pier. The opposite side of the road is a holidaymaker's paradise full of Amusement arcades, ice cream parlours, fish and chip shops and restaurants, pubs, and gift shops. The crab stalls alongside the fish pier were leased from the council; and run by the families of the local fishing community, each individual crab stall had been in the same family for quite a number of years. All the fish and shellfish on the stalls were caught fresh by the fishermen's own fishing craft, and sold on the stall the next day by their families.

A popular cheap shellfish for the holidaymaker were winkles, sold in paper bags with a complementary small pin provided. Winkles then grew in abundance in the many rock pools on the North and South Bays, but to pick them was a time-consuming job. The fishermen were only too pleased to accept your offer to supply them with the winkles; they would even provide you with a small Hessian sack. However, the sack would have to be completely filled with the winkles, for which you were given the payment of ten shillings a sack, (50 pence) but to fill that small sack was nearly a full day's backbreaking work. We would start enthusiastically early in the morning, and begin picking the winkles from the rocks with great speed, but as the day wore on our hands became sore, and that early enthusiasm soon began to wane. It was as though the sack had an endless bottom, for no matter how many winkles you put into the sack it never seemed full, and to claim your money the astute fishermen insisted on a very full sack. After many hours of hard work and aching backs, we would heave the heavy sacks onto our trolleys, and then return to the fishermen's baiting sheds, and our well-earned reward. The winkles were washed and boiled, ready for sale on the crab stalls for the eager visitors the next day. Winkle picking although rewarding was not a job to be done every day. Not only was it extremely hard work but it did not leave us much time to enjoy the school holidays. Besides, there were other far easier and more pleasant jobs to acquire.

Working with the donkeys on the beach in the summer holidays was a much-coveted job, but a job that rarely came up. However, one night I learned that one of the regular boys had been taken to hospital that evening with tonsillitis. Eager to take his place, I was waiting on the beach early the next morning for the donkey's arrival. The donkey owner agreed to give me a one-day's trial for 3 shillings (15 pence) and if suitable the job was to be mine for the rest of the season. There were usually six donkeys and three boys who, with the owner set off early every morning to take the donkeys from their overnight stables to the beach about two miles away. The same route was repeated on the return journey in the evening. The attraction of the work was that not only were we being paid for the work, but also we were allowed to ride on one of the donkeys; both to the beach and back home again A stick with a white rag was stuck in the sand away from the crowded beach, approximately 50 yards from the donkeys starting place, this was the route of the donkeys ride, although the donkeys knew by instinct when to turn around and return back. The owner, with a big leather purse strapped around his waist would take the sixpence fare (two and a half pence) from the line of young children eagerly waiting their turn for a ride. For safety reasons a boy accompanied each donkey with its young passenger, and each boy had two donkeys in his charge. Each of the donkeys had a name which was displayed on a red band strapped across the donkey's forehead. The owner informed me that my two charges for the day were to be Darky and Mary, however, much to my annoyance the information seemed to amuse the other two boys, but I just ignored them. The three of us set off in a line on our first trek of the day, the two other boys kept looking at me, exchanging glances with each other. Unconcerned, and full of enthusiasm, I took my first walk with Darky. Darky plodded slowly in a straight line towards the turning point then he turned around and headed back, with his beaming young passenger, while I walked proudly by their side. As we returned to the starting point, the other three donkeys stood waiting with their eager young passengers smiling excitedly. The other two boys began to walk with their charges, but Mary, looking defiantly at me, refused to move until the owner gave her a smack on her rump. For the first few yards Mary plodded slowly forward, but then she began to veer closer towards the near side of the crowded beach. The owner screeched out for me to keep her walking in a straight line, while the other two boys exchanged knowing looks and sniggering. For the rest of the morning the pattern was the same. While Darky was always obedient and dependable, Mary was stubborn and unpredictable, one minute she was calm and responsive, the next she would trot quickly away or suddenly stop and refuse to move at all, or drift away from the well-trodden track regardless of any pleading or coaxing on my part. The other boys enjoyed my predicament, while the owner shouted a few choice words.

By mid-noon the sun was shining brightly and much to my relief Mary seemed to have passed over her rebellious stage, as she plodded slowly up and down the course diligently. However, I was lulled into a false security. On one return journey; with a little boy on her back, Mary without warning suddenly veered quickly off the well-worn track, and headed towards the crowded part of the beach, and regardless of my pleading and pulling, she plodded quickly towards a group of people sitting in their deckchairs eating their packed lunches. Mary stopped directly in front of them and emptied her bladder. The holidaymakers jumped up in disgust, protesting loudly while the little boy sitting on Mary's back looked on in open-mouthed surprise. I managed to divert Mary back on to her route, but only after a few more choice words from the owner, who was hollering at me from the starting position, Mary thankfully was obedient for the rest of the afternoon. It was early evening and the beach began to slowly empty, the hungry, and red-faced holidaymakers began to pack up, preparing to disperse to their various guesthouses for their evening meal, or their return journey back home. Business had been brisk all through the day, but now the donkeys stood waiting patiently in a line ready to for the long walk back to their stables and their supper. Just then a little girl approached the donkeys holding her mother's hand, and pointing, she walked directly up to Mary. The little girl's mother; after paying the owner the fare, gently lifted the little girl up onto Mary's saddle, and she held onto her as we began to walk down the track. All was well until the return journey, when Mary's pace quickened and she began to divert from the track, and regardless of all my shouting and pulling, Mary trotted towards the now less crowded beach. The girl's mother looked at me in concern as I tried to divert Mary back onto her route, however Mary had other ideas. Mary approached a man and his little boy, who together were proudly building a magnificent looking fort constructed out of sand. Mary stopped abruptly next to them and emptied her steaming bowels, directly into the centre of the fort. Suddenly there was mayhem, the boy burst into tears, the boy's father jumped up furiously, waving a small spade at me, and screeching abuse. The little girl's mother and the donkey owner, who had suddenly appeared, also shouted furiously at me. The only one not concerned was the little girl who was still sitting on Mary's back; giggling happily. Perhaps I was mistaken; but through all the mayhem going on around me, I could have sworn that Mary with her back to me slowly turned her head around, looked at me, and winked. Needless to say, I failed my one day's trial pathetically, but what annoyed me the most was the fact that I did not get paid, but more importantly even get a free ride on a donkey.

Saturday and especially Sunday, William Street coach park was full to overflowing during the summer months; coaches were even parked in the nearby streets. The coaches began arriving from early morning onwards from all over Yorkshire and the North East. The day-trippers, after departing from their coaches, bright and chirpy, streamed in their hundreds down the steep hills leading to the beaches. However, during the afternoon an eerie silence surround the deserted coaches, until early teatime, when in small dribbles at first, and then in swarming crowds, the red-faced holidaymakers wearily started their way back to their awaiting coaches. For the next few hours the coach park was awash with noise and bustle as the visitors boarded the coaches, and then one by one the filled coaches began their return journeys back home. By early evening council workmen began the task of clearing up some of the scattered litter, while small gangs of boys ahead of the workmen, eagerly collected the empty lemonade bottles for the returnable deposits. But we were unconcerned, for it was later on in the evening that the real bonanza occurred.

By dusk the coach park was nearly deserted, and most of the litter cleared. All that remained were a few empty coaches, their passengers were usually inebriated males from a working man's club, or work outings, then they would slowly and nosily begin to appear, staggering and singing as they approached their dimly lit coaches. Waiting until one coach was nearly full, we would then climb inside and ask.

"Would anybody like a song?

Always, without doubt, the cheering merry answer would be a resounding

"Yesss, come on lads. Give us a song"

The five of us would then sing, although a bit out of tune "She'll be coming round the Mountain" Followed by 'The Happy Wanderer'. Unconcerned at our out of tune warbling, the men merrily began clapping and singing along with us. As the two songs finished, amid all the clapping and shouting, we would then would push Sam to the front of us to sing his solo. For all his dimness and looks, Sam had a very soulful singing voice. The song he always sung was; "My Papa" the first two lines went---

"Oh, my Papa, to me he was so wonderful. Oh, my Papa to me he was so good----."

A strange choice of a song, considering Sam's own brutal treatment by his drunken father. However, Sam's lilting voice, coupled with his mish mash of clothing, and his single lens glasses, gave the song a poignant touch that seemed to reach out to the now nostalgic and mostly silent audience. As soon as Sam had ceased singing the men would shout and clap enthusiastically, and usually one of them taking off his flat cap, and holding it out with his hand would shout out loudly

"Come on lads, dig b----- deep for the young uns."

After collecting the proceeds, we would then repeat the whole performance again on the next coaches. Much later, under the hazy glow of a street gas lamp we would divide the proceeds five ways, which sometimes came to about one pound each, a fortune for us in those days. (Oh, by the way That is how Dave and I became the proud owners of those rayon swimming trunks) but more importantly, it gave Sam not just an equal share of the kitty, but also a little self-respect, and a feeling that at long last being an important member of the gang.

One year on our last week of a scorching summer school holiday, a group of six boys, Dave and I included, had acquired a week's work of potato picking for a local potato merchant situated in Seamer, a village a few miles outside Scarborough. Eager and excited on a very early warm Monday morning Dave and I boarded the early bus for the potato merchant's office, situated just on the outskirts of the village. Assembled in the merchant's yard were a group of eight men and women, plus our group of excited young boys. A tubby stern looking, elderly man dressed in a checked three-piece suit and sporting a trilby hat, approached us, and after writing down our names he abruptly ordered everybody to climb aboard two flat back trailers that were attached to a tractor apiece. On one of the trailers tied up tightly at the back, was a metal bin with a lid. As the tractors slowly spluttered out of the yard and onto the outside village road all the boys chatted excitedly amongst ourselves, for not only were we going to do a full week's paid work, but we were outside our own comfort zone, and although the village was only about six miles from Scarborough for us it could have been in a foreign country. Five minutes later the tractors pulled off the main road and onto a narrow dusty sun-baked track, passing a number of wheat fields on the way. Although all of the boys chatted and fooled around while sitting on the trailers, the older men and women stayed silent, and smiled condescendingly at us, obviously knowing what laid ahead. Suddenly the tractors pulled into a gated field and then came to an abrupt halt. A slim, weather beaten faced man, jumped off one of the trailers, and bawled for everyone to follow, while he opened the gate. The man then strode quickly down the field, and started to knock sticks into the sun-baked soil, on one side of the field, about three metres apart. The two tractors were disconnected from their trailers and three of the men released and lowered the bin to the ground, and tipped the water inside the bin into another bin with a lid, while the other tractor drove away from the field. The remaining tractor was fastened up to a large spiked wheel device near the gate opening. The man giving the orders returned, and turning to all the boys he explained that he was the foreman, and he informed us in a harsh voice that.

"There will be no mucking about, we were paid to work, and b------- work we would."

He then placed each boy with two men or women and pointed to which staked off section of the field we were all required to work on. The tractor, attached with its rolled spiked appliance, rode down one furrow of the long field, turning over the hard-baked soil, and exposing the buried potatoes, the tractor then returned back up the next furrow doing the same, while each person frantically gathered up the potatoes in their section into a wired basket that was provided. When your basket was filled you then emptied the basket into a deep box, which the Forman and another man tipped the box into a high sided trailer at the side of the field. The section seemed endless, and although you followed the tractor quickly, by the time you had picked your potatoes on one furrow, the tractor had reappeared at the next furrow, leaving little time for conversation, never mind resting. Our mothers had packed Dave and I up with sandwiches, a bottle of pop, and a tin mug apiece, however you were only allowed a drink of water from the butt at a ten minute break, one in the morning and one in the afternoon, plus a drink at a half hour lunch break, you were allowed to drink as much water as you wanted at those times, but there was no time to drink in between the breaks. The water was stored in the metal water bin at the top of the field which was toped up the following morning. We had left home at six thirty am and returned home at about six thirty pm, very tired, tanned, and dust ingrained. The days were hot, the work was hard, and we had little time for fun or banter. Each day, we returned to the same field but by the third day only Dave and I still remained from the original eight boys who had started the week in such high hopes and high spirits. Both of our dads had insisted that if the work was too much, we were to pack the job in, however Dave and I were determined to finish the full weeks work. The week's work ended on the Friday night, and we were told to come back to the office in the yard on Saturday morning to collect our pay. Although later I was to have a paper round and then a job as a delivery boy before starting work as a fully paid apprentice bricklayer, nothing gave me more satisfaction and sense of achievement than when I proudly held that first brown pay packet in my hand. Dave and I had earned two pounds and ten shillings (two pounds fifty pence) each, this seemed like a fortune to us at the time. When I returned home that Saturday morning and proudly showed mum and dad my wage packet, I was taken by complete surprise when dad had replied

"Keep the money son, you've dam well-earned it, go and treat yourself."

71

All through the summer months, there were various other little jobs and scams on the go, too numerous to recall. This may seem mercenary at such an early age, but has I have already stated we were far too young for any official work, and as we received no pocket money, to afford any sort of treats, everything required hard work. However we never missed out on enjoying ourselves and there was always time for adventures and excitement, also there was a fun side to any work. There is an old Yorkshire saying that I recall,

'You don't get owt for nowt.'

Simply meaning if you want something you must work for it, and that saying to me is just as relevant today as it was back in those early days.

CHAPTER 4

THE DAY TRIPPERS

From the mid-fifties to the early seventies, the traditional British seaside holiday was at the peak of its popularity, and I was fortunate to have spent my formative years growing up in Scarborough, 'The Queen of the Yorkshire Coast'

The Scarborough coastline has two bays. The North Bay, with its boating lake, putting greens and a quaint miniature railway that transports you on a gentle journey through a leafy wood, past a children's boating pond and then around the grass lined cliff tops which overlook a large and peaceful beach. The North Bay was unhurried and calm, with no gaudy noisy amusement arcades, or the greasy smell of fish and chip shops within a two-mile radius, however a few shops and cafes did sell ice cream, waffles, cold and hot drinks and other light refreshments, while families had the vast beach and cluster of rocks to play on and explore. The older generation could enjoy a relaxing game of bowls on the green adjacent to the old Edwardian theatre, the 'Floral Hall', or take an afternoons nap on the lines of wooden benches in Peasholm Park, while listening to a brass band performing from a covered stage in the middle of the idyllic boating lake, or take a stroll up the tree and bush lined Glen, with its slowly babbling stream, and a pleasant, children's boating pond.

However, The South Bay was a complete contrast, it was the 'Las Vegas' of the North East Coast. A cauldron of noise, colours, and smells, that mixed with the salt sea air wafting around the many amusement arcades, fish and chip restaurants, ice cream parlours, gift shops and crab stalls. Incoming pleasure boats, the Coronia, Regal Lady, and The Yorkshire Lady, blasted out their sirens, while on their varnished wooden decks their fare paying passengers waved to the next batch of excited passengers waiting patiently on the crowded quayside of the pier. Fishermen standing at the top of the slip way of the fishing harbour, touted the visitors to ride in their motor boats for a 'Trip around the Bay.'

During the week the early rising holidaymakers could stroll around the ancient fish pier with all its noise and bustle, watching in total fascination as the local fishing boats unloaded their night's bounty onto the wet slippery cobbled fishing quay. All species of fish, iced and packed in open wooden boxes, stared out in a wide-eyed gaze of crystal horror, as the auctioneers assistant slapped a ticket onto a fish merchants successful bid. Black shelled lobsters, their once lethal claws now bound with string, moved in a slow throe of death in large wooden crates, their fate? Bound for the rich gourmets table. By midmorning, a steady stream of holidaymakers strolled down the steep narrow roads leading towards the beaches, after partaking of their ritual 'Full English breakfast' from the many hotels and guesthouses scattered around the town. Foreshore Road on the South Bay runs for approximately half a mile along the seafront, effectively dividing the beach from the many amenities, amusements, gift shops, and cafés. It was a half mile of bright lights and waffling aromas, giving out an air of expectation to entice you to indulge and enjoy yourself, and none more so typified the feel and spirit of the British seaside than the typical weekend holidaymaker; 'The Day Trippers.'

The packed coaches began to arrive at the two huge coach parks on William Street, and Valley Road, early Sunday morning. By midday, both coach parks would be full to overflowing, people arriving from as far as Newcastle and Sunderland on the north east coast, to Leeds and Sheffield in the heart of the West and South Yorkshire, and all the other towns' in between. Parents and children, grandparents, groups of young men and women, all began their slow walk down to the foreshore like pilgrims in search of the Holy Grail. On their way down the steep and narrow roads and footpaths leading to the beach, groups of young men and women would stop outside one of the many fully stocked gift shops and bazaars, laughing and sniggering at the saucy picture postcards on open display in the shop windows, while outside on the pavement a collection of items were for sale, plastic bucket and spades, children's swimming costumes and trunks, or small deep buckets containing bamboo sticks with a small fishing nets fastened at the end. Some of the youths and young women would come out of the shops after maybe purchasing a pair of sunglasses, or one of the black cowboy hats with the cheeky 'Kiss Me Quick' emblazed on the front, equipped and ready for the days fun ahead. By midday the heaving seafront was a kaleidoscope of sights and sounds. Families and the elderly queued on the sandy beach, eager to hire their pastel coloured stripped deckchairs, before seeking out a piece of precious space on the swarming sands. Groups of teenagers and young courting couples, walked along the promenade and piers, licking their ice cream cornets while absorbing all the sights and sounds with relish. Bingo stall attendants called out; trying to entice punters into their bingo stalls, with cries.

"Come on in and enjoy yourself, only one win and you can take your pick from the bottom shelf, or if you like; you can save up your winning tickets for the bigger prizes on the higher shelves."

Gangs of boisterous youths joked and cajoled with each other in the noisy amusement arcades, showing off their skills on a shooting gallery, or on one of the many brightly lit games on display; while children and older people tried their luck on the vast array of penny slot machines lined on every wall of the amusement arcades At the very top end of Foreshore Road approaching the Spa, was 'Gala Land.' The tall, wooden entrance with its black and white posters and photo's festooned around four wide wooden piers, enticed the public to engage in its mixed entertainment. A steep flight of wooden steps leading down from the road brought you to the underground entrance, where, after paying the sixpence (two and a half pence) admission charge; there to greet you was a small middle aged man dressed in the bright coloured silk clothes, and cap, of a jockey, who with a whip in his hand, would, for the price of one shilling (5p) guess your weight, before asking you to step onto a large weighing machine and confirm his usual accurate prediction, then he would give you a small memento. The inside of Gala Land was like stepping into a forgone age. The walls were the actual sandstone rock that had been gouged out many years before to create the underground amusement park. All the old penny slot machines played Victorian scenes, a marching army band, a hospital laundry, and a priest reading from a bible as a blindfolded prisoner, with a noose around his neck descended through an open trap door. Also, on display was the original saucy 'What the butler saw' machines with their metal viewing slots. Among the dark old-fashioned varied stalls was the 'Fortune Teller', a leather skinned Gypsy woman with a headscarf, and dressed in a flowing dress, her ears adorned with huge gold earrings, sitting in her dimly lit cavern, looking like she had been there for a hundred years. While on a raised stage, in a seated small auditorium there would be a ladies' string quartet, playing chamber music at set time sessions, or a small band playing old popular tunes. Occasionally in the auditorium a children's talent contest would be held. A track half way up the walls carried small carriages around the hall.   At the far end of the underground wonderland a small Helter Skelter stood, where children climbed up the wooden staircase, coconut mat in hand, and then slid down the well-worn slide. Next to the Helter Skelter was an old dodgem car circuit, with equally old dodgem cars bumping and colliding into each other. Fittingly at the rear of the dark cavern a more sinister small wax work museum was situated, consisting of old known murderers, whose bright waxen faces seemed more haunting in the dim light.   And to complement those early century scenes, wild birds flew haphazardly all around the vast cavern like demon bats. But, for all its eccentricity Gala Land was a popular draw for the visitors and residents alike, especially on a blustery wet summer day.

At the opposite end of Foreshore Road is the beginning of the Marine Drive that leads to the more sedate North Bay. Situated at the foot of the ancient castle a small fun park adjoined the far pier, with open slatted floorboards, supported on huge wooden pillars set deep into the seabed below. Games of family fun, and penny slot machines were in abundance, with the visitors queuing eagerly to take rides on the Helter Skelter, and the turning, dipping, Dive Bomber. Teenage girls screeched in terror as the two seated cockpit at each end of the giant arm spun and propelled around as it turned in a fast turning circle At the entrance to the fun park was the popular dodgem track. Excited screams and yells, filled the air as the dumpy cars raced around the thick shiny canvas floor, sparks flying from the top of the metal rods on the back of the cars that scraped   along the wired mesh ceiling, and scurried haphazardly; bumping and colliding into each other On the crowded beach, young children would act out their fantasies building sand castles and forts, with buckets and spades, whooping with delight as they ran back and forth to the sea edge, dodging small waves to fill their small tin or plastic buckets with seawater. Donkeys slowly plodded up and down the beach with their young excited passengers. Older men and women with their trousers and skirts hitched up to their knees, paddled on the water's edge, while in the open crowded bay small sailing crafts crossed each other in perpetual motion, leaving behind wisps of white trails in the dark green water. Food and snacks were in abundance, ice cream wafer sandwiches, or ice cream cornets topped with a Cadbury's flake. Chips and freshly caught Scarborough cod or haddock in a golden crispy batter, eaten inside one of the many cafés with tea, bread and butter, or served outside in grease proof bags and white paper wrapping, eaten either with your fingers or with a small wooden fork. Crowds stood on the pavement watching in fascination as assistants in white overalls rolled, cut, and made the many items in 'The Rock Shop' with all manners of colours, flavours, and shapes, all for sale and encased in the glassed fronted counter. On the opposite side of the road the local fishing fraternity proudly displayed their family names in huge letters on the many crab stalls, offering all kinds of sea food, shrimps, cockles, prawns, oysters and winkles, and of course crabs in their shells, or dressed with a sprig of parsley and wrapped in cellophane. Small wooden boxes of local oak smoked kippers could be purchased and posted to your home and savoured at leisure. At teatime red faced but happy, the day-trippers began their slow weary trek back up the steep hills to the coach parks, carrying the customary

Scarborough lettered rock and other souvenirs from their day at the seaside. By early evening only a few lonely coaches stood waiting patiently for their passengers, usually groups of men on a works, or club outing, whose ray of sunshine that day had been in the many pints, and bottles of beer that they had consumed with pleasure in the seafront public houses. Time unfortunately moves on, and those halcyon days of my early childhood like the hoards of day trippers have faded into the past. The thriving fishing industry is now much smaller, along with all its characters. The amusement arcades, once so much fun on a sunny afternoon, or a welcome haven on a summer's wet day for family entertainment, now only offers machines to gamble for financial gain, or games only an Einstein could understand. However, the British summer holiday is still alive and well, fish and chips and all, but now alas on the sunnier coastal lines of Spain.

CHAPTER 5

SEASONS, EVENTS, AND HAPPENINGS

Throughout the year and in each season, there was always a date, an event, or a time to enjoy. I have tried to convey the excitement and atmosphere of those events which I can still vividly recall.

PANCAKE DAY

Shrove Tuesday or better known as 'Pancake Day' took place in early February on the seafront of The South Bay. The origins dated back to the previous early centuries, when the day before Lent any food left in the house were utilised and used up before fasting began. The ingredients were mixed together and fried on an open fire, from those early beginnings this evolved into the frying of the modern day 'pancake' Originally Shrove Tuesday did not begin until the ancient curfew bell, now in the Rotunda Museum at the top end of Foreshore Road, was rung at precisely twelve noon, a signal for housewives to commence to use all the leftover food. After the meal the people (at the time the fishing community) would then assemble on the seafront to take part in games of fun before their final feast which marked the beginning of Lent. But by the time I was growing up, Shrove Tuesday was signified with eating pancakes and skipping on Foreshore Road. After the summer season all the amusements, crab stalls, and the other amenities had closed down until the following summer, leaving the Foreshore virtually deserted for the winter months. Shrove Tuesday was also a half term holiday for the local schools. Although the vast majority of amenities and shops in the town remained open. However, in the 'Bottom End 'Foreshore Road was closed to traffic for the annual Shrove Tuesday celebrations. After lunch crowds of women, and children began to assemble on the seafront. Some of the young girls brought their own skipping ropes, while the boys began playing football or other games on the beach until the 'REAL' skipping commenced. The majority of the adults, mostly women, stood patiently on both sides of the road; waiting for the fishermen to bring the long thick skipping ropes. The ropes, approximately twenty or thirty millimetres in diameter, and long enough to span the road were actually used to tie up the various fishing craft to the piers. It required a strong armed man at each end to swing the heavy rope. As the ropes slowly gathered momentum the anticipating skippers began to drift into the swinging arc of the ropes. Soon the seafront was awash with lines of laughing and shouting adults, and children skipping across the width of foreshore Road. Even the foul winter weather or the roaring North Sea could not dampen the enthusiasm of the crowds. As early evening dusk began to fill the murky grey February sky; the crowds slowly began to disperse, weary but happy, and ravenous in anticipation for their pancakes. Arriving home, mum began to mix and cook the hoards of light delicious pancakes. A bowl of sugar, and Jif, a plastic lemon filled with lemon juice, stood waiting on the table, ready for spreading across the pancakes. But my own favourite spread on the pancakes was the tin of Lyles treacle that dad heated up on the gas stove, which when liquefied he picked up from the stove very carefully, and placed on to a saucer, and I spooned it very generously over the pancakes.

THE HERRING SEASON

During the six weeks of the school summer holidays boredom was a word we seldom used. There was always something to occupy our lively minds. However, although there were so many things to do, without doubt the most anticipated time of the holidays were the later weeks of August which herald the approach of 'The 'Herring Season'.

The Herring season had been an event in the Scarborough harbour for nearly one hundred years. The huge shoals of herring began their epic journey from around the east coast of Scotland, before swimming down the entire east coast of England, with the shoals increasing in size day by day. The herring were relentlessly pursued by the weather beaten; hard working Scottish fishermen in their Drifters (a larger fishing boat than the local Keel boat) The Drifters fished throughout the night, disgorging their huge cargoes of herring early the next morning at the nearest fishing port. Waiting in anticipation were the 'Herring girls'. These girls had travelled all the way down from Scotland from port to port to cut and gut the loads of herring on the quaysides, that were unloaded from the boats, and place them into large barrels, the girls were a happy attraction to the summer visitors. The days of the old steam trawlers and the 'Herring girls' had faded in to history when I was a boy, but Scarborough at the time was still a major fishing port, with a thriving fishing community, and had its own assembly of fishing craft berthed in its harbour. As the herring shoals approached Scarborough the local keel boats joined forces with the Scottish contingent for the following weeks, until the shoals of herring moved further down the coast. The days before the herring shoals appeared, we would diligently scour the many rock pools around both bays, for any sign of herring sile, the small fish that the herring fed on, a sure sign that the herring were on their way. Suddenly, like an invading army the herring shoals arrived, and for the next few weeks the Harbour was a cauldron of noise, excitement, and action. From early dawn the drifters and keel boats entered the harbour and tied up to the crowded quayside, a flurry of expectation rippled around the harbour as more and more boats entered the harbour, eager to unload their nights bounty. The fish pier would be crammed to the limit with Drifters and Keel boats, and the middle pier was also brought into action, to ease the demand for berths.

On the middle pier, large Lorries with open backs and dozens of empty metal barrels parked at the edge of the quay side, ready and waiting to fill the barrels with the night's catches.

The crew of each boat usually stood in the 'Keep' below the deck, where the herring had been stored overnight, throwing and shovelling the mass of herrings into large wicker baskets which were then hoisted up by hand from the keeps by a pulley on the boat, and tipped into the empty bins of the waiting lorries. The lorry drivers quickly upended the cane baskets into the empty steel barrels and returned the empty baskets back down to the keep, in the process some of the herring would spill on to the decks of the Lorries which the drivers would kick onto the quay side with gay abandon. Both the fishing and the middle piers were a hive of noise and activity as the fishermen and their helpers cajoled to each other in broad Scottish; and Yorkshire banter. Large crowds of locals and visitors, watched in fascination, while dozens of seagulls plodded along the slippery fish scaled piers, gorging themselves on the glut of discarded herring. As the fully loaded Lorries heaved their way up the steep roads leading from the foreshore, herrings would spill out from the overfilled open barrels and onto the road, and the herring that laid scattered on the quay floors and open road were accepted as free game. In eager excitement our gang, with numerous other schoolboys, would gather up the overspills. For the next few weeks, from early dawn, the whole daily process would be repeated. After watching all the arrivals and activities of the boats and the shouting and joking of the unloading, we would gather up as much of the discarded fish that we could carry, then take them home to be cooked and eaten by our families and neighbours, or sometimes sell them to the watching visitors

Sam Dawson and his family perhaps more than most looked forward to the herring season, simply because it would mean that for once there would be plenty to eat for their undernourished stomachs. Sam's dad would rub his hands in anticipation, but not for the same good intensions. Sam's dad, like a modern-day Fagin, sat smoking cigarettes in his tiny squalid back yard while his wife, sons, and even daughters, returned from the piers with their free morning's gatherings. After threading the herring with string through their gills, in bunches of six, he would send his off spring around the neighbourhood touting the herring for a few pence. All the money collected; he would take for himself for his sacred beer and fags, but Sam and his brothers and sisters, always managed to keep a few pence back to give to their mum. Gradually the huge shoals of herring moved further down the coast and the harbour began to return back to normality, by which time the initial delight and taste of fried, steamed, or pickled herring had worn very thin. But of course, there would always be the following year to anticipate.

At the time, so much herring was in abundance that nobody could have foreseen that in less than ten years' time the herring would become to near extension, due to the modern day technology of radar, which did away with the many years of experienced fishing men pinpointing where the huge shoals of fish might be, but mainly it was the mass invasion of the large foreign trawlers drawn to our coasts, which hovered up not only the many species of fish, but their traditional feeding grounds on the sea bed as well, and in the process nearly desecrated the British fishing industry, which has been almost finished off by the European bureaucrats.

BONFIRE NIGHT

From September until Christmas was a long bleak time. The days grew shorter and the dark nights became longer, while the weather became colder. But with the approach of November there was excitement in the air and a date to remember; 'Bonfire Night.' The event was in recognition of Guy Fawkes and his fellow plotters executions, when over three centuries previously the plotters were burned at the stake for a failed attempt to blow up the Houses of Parliament. However the meaning meant nothing to us, for although we were aware of the facts, the excitement and fun of Bonfire night, and the days leading up to the event was all that occupied our minds.

About a week before bonfire night, all over Scarborough piles of burnable rubbish began to appear on waste grounds, spare lands, and the two beaches, all gathered by eager schoolboys and girls, for their own gangs bonfire`s. But the largest bonfire by far every year was on William Street coach park. Children and older boys and girls came from all over town; and for this one occasion they were amalgamated into one single gang, with the sole purpose of gathering as much burnable refuse as possible. For my mates and myself there was an added incentive because William Street was in our own playing area.

In the town itself every shop, business, and work place, were visited with the eager but simple request.

"Have you any bonfire rubbish please?"

The request would be greeted with a warm response and not the usual harsh unhelpful reply when seeking any assistance, however the willingness to help was not always because of good intensions on the their part, but because it gave the shop keepers and businesses a chance to clear out their premises of any unwanted materials; that cluttered up their shops and stores, and in the process for all the surplus rubbish to be carried away free of charge by eager young boys. After school the streets were filled each night with boys and some girls carting and carrying rubbish in all sorts of makeshift old prams and barrows, or by hand. William Street resembled a large ant colony, for besides the major bonfire a number of small individual bonfires also began to appear as gangs of boys and girls scurried back and forth with their bounties. All manner of unwanted rubbish was collected, ranging from cardboard and wooden boxes, discarded bicycle and car tyres, old wooden doors, furnishings, used books and old documents, along with all sorts of other unwanted burnable rubbish, which was then carted away and tipped at the base of the bonfires. Each group would diligently sift through their own collections to sort out any useful items, before tossing the useless ones onto the growing piles of rubbish. On one occasion a tobacconist gave us a number of cardboard boxes filled with various brands of cigarette, cigar, and tobacco advertisements and signs. As we sifted through the boxes Sam let out a large yell and excitedly began to show the rest of us a small wooden box he had unearthed, it was full of individually wrapped cigars that the shop keeper had obviously overlooked. On the basis of finders keepers we had no hesitation in dividing the contents between the five of us. Eric, Dave, and myself, decided to take the cigars home for our dad's enjoyment, but Pete, trying to prove he was more daring and grown up than the rest of us swaggered up to a gang of much older boys who were smoking cigarettes. He put a cigar in his mouth and brazenly asked for a light. The youths at first just stared at Pete, and then one of them smiling, stepped forward with a box of matches and lit Pete's cigar. Pete nodded cockily at the older boy, and inhaled deeply on the cigar a few times and began coughing, before turning back towards us and grinning. A few seconds later he suddenly withdrew the cigar from his mouth and began coughing and retching. The youth, along with his mates, roared with laughter as they menacingly circled around Pete, and with threats they ordered Pete to carry on smoking the cigar. Pete, still coughing; and now with a deathly pall on his face, reluctantly began drawing on the cigar once more, all the while the older boys were chanting for him to inhale deeper and deeper. Pete, his face turning a ghastly white, and his eyes all but disappearing, staggered forward, whipped the cigar from his mouth, and violently vomited all over one of the youths, before putting his hand around his mouth and crying, he then ran across the Coach park back home. Meanwhile Sam, always on the lookout to make a few pence approached the older boys and displayed his cigars, before asking if anyone wanted to buy his cigars for two shilling (ten pence). The boys scoffed, and to Sam's dismay promptly snatched the cigars from his hands and walked away laughing. Unfortunate for Sam the whole episode had been witnessed by one of his elder sisters who duly reported the incident to their dad. The next day Sam was sporting a bruised lip and a thick ear given to him from a scrounging, furious dad. Besides the shopkeepers and other businesses, bonfire night also gave the householders a chance to clear out their homes of any unwanted rubbish. If the items were too large or heavy for the householders to bring to the bonfires themselves; there was no shortage of willing volunteers to help remove the items. Broken settee's, worn out armchairs, wooden tables and chairs, and old mattresses began to appear on the bonfires along with smaller burnable rubbish.

With just a day left before the big event the collecting of rubbish began to ease, but no one could relax, for the evenings always brought the threat of bonfire raiding. Bonfire raiding was looked upon as both a dare, and a quick and easy way of adding to your own stockpile. Sometimes the bonfires would be heavily guarded in which case a skirmish would take place. However, the threat of raiders held no fears for the bonfires on William Street, because every night the coach park was alive with young boys and older youths. While some of the young boys like ourselves, played games, the older youths stood around in groups talking and smoking, or baking potatoes in the many small fires dotted around the coach park. Groups of girls would appear, and some of the youths with guitars or mouth organs, would strum and play the latest pop songs of the day, tempting the other older boys and girls to join in singing, although most of the songs were sung out of tune, or sometimes with the wrong words, nobody seemed to care.

The night before the main event was known as 'Mischievous Night' and as the name suggests, although unofficial, many pranks were played. Seeking any empty milk bottles left on a door step, with a piece of paper inserted in one of the bottles, perhaps asking for a extra pint of milk for the next morning, the paper would be removed and rewritten asking for six extra bottles of milk. We also found great amusement by running down a street and knocking on every door on the way, laughing at the angry response as the disturbed householders appeared cursing us from their doorsteps. Or fastening a piece of string onto the door knobs of two adjoin houses and then knock loudly on each door, laughing as the two householders shouted and strained against each other trying to open their doors. Sometimes we would smear the door handle with treacle and knock loudly on the door, then hide as the householder came out to answer. Angry and frustrated the householder stepped outside looking for the perpetrators, and returning back in doors, they would grip the smeared outside door handle.

By teatime on bonfire night, the main bonfire on William Street was gigantic, dwarfing the smaller ones by at least three or four meters. A number of weeks previous to the day many newsagents, and toy shops had fireworks on display and with no age restrictions then, you could buy them. They could be purchased singly or in boxes of mixed varieties, the boxes might contain a spinning wheel, a rocket, and a mixture of fireworks that would cascade into brightly coloured flames or sparks. Some of the shops ran a fireworks club in which weeks before you could save up your money for bonfire night, and any money made by running errands odd jobs etc, you deposited the money into your fireworks account at the shop. Later the money value on the cards would be exchanged to purchase the fireworks of your choice. However, for most boys our sparse savings was saved for only one type of firework; 'the Penny Banger.' No pretty colours and sparks, spinning wheels, or rockets for us. Not only did you get more bangers for your money; but you also had more fun. You would light the fuse of the banger; put it under a empty tin or box, then stand back, and when the banger exploded; the tin or box would usually jump into the air, or you could simply light the banger and hold it for as long as possible in your hand before tossing it up in the air and watch it explode. Throwing bangers against rival boys, could erupt into a 'banger fight, although the stupidity and danger was not apparent to us at the time, even after a passing adult warned 'You`ll have somebody`s eye out doing that.'. Shortly after teatime the smaller bonfires were lit. But not before the obligated Guy Fawkes was perched at the top of the bonfire. A discarded coat or jumper and old trousers were stuffed with rags and newspaper, the sleeves and bottom of the trousers tied together before a cardboard mask was placed over a turnip and fixed to the torso as a head, finally an old cap or hat was fastened on the Guy Fawkes head, then the finished effigy eagerly placed at the top of the bonfire. As the small bonfires burned, rockets zoomed high into the coal black sky before exploding into multicoloured stars. All over the Scarborough sky line shades of bright colours cascaded, mingled with the acrid smell of smoke coming from the bonfires, while the loud cracks and small explosions from the endless bangers and rockets echoed in the cold night air. The smaller children made swirling star shapes by twirling around the sparklers they were holding in their gloved hands, of course; overseen by their ever-present parents.

At last the gigantic bonfire was set ablaze by a number of older youths who attacked the monstrous heap from all sides with blazing torches, watched by wide eyed children, adults, and teenagers, and the ever watchful eyes of a couple of policemen. The huge bonfire with its Guy Fawkes perched at the summit soon took hold as it snarled and crackled into life, lighting up the whole area of William Street. The heat from the fire became so overwhelming that step by step the gaping crowd stood further and further back. While the big bonfire had yet to reach its peak, the smaller ones had began to diminish rapidly, yet as the night wore on William Street was still a cauldron of noise and colours, overseen by the blazing giant.

By midnight, except for a few youths the crowds had all but disappeared, and the local fire brigade toured the town dismantling, and dowsing down the subdued fires. The next morning the spectacle of the night before was an anticlimax, for the small bonfires were now just a sodden disjointed sorry looking mess in the early morning light. The big bonfire, although ravaged and pulled aside, by the Fire Brigade still smouldered defiantly and would do so for a few more days, helped by willing young hands until the local council came and removed away all the debris, and so officially 'Bonfire Night'. Had ended.

THE TANNER RUSH

At the time movies, or the pictures as we called them, was at the height of its popularity. Although a boy or girl had to be accompanied by an adult to watch the main pictures. However, for the children there was always the Saturday matinee show. There were two Picture houses that held a Saturday matinee show, The Odeon at the top end of Scarborough's main street, a matinee was held there every Saturday morning. The Odeon club badge were given for you to wear showing that you were a member. The matinee consisted of a number of cartoons, and a couple of educational films followed by a short intermission. Then an adult member of staff, or a older youth or girl came on stage, as the M.C and Birthdays sometimes were announced. A demonstration, such as how to use the latest craze such as a yo yo, a hula hoop, or how to make patterns from folding pieces of paper. The morning show ending with a serial, perhaps one more cartoon and a short comic film.

But it was the Saturday afternoon matinee show, held at the Futurist theatre and picture, house that we eagerly anticipated. The Futurist was situated at the bottom of Blands Cliff on Foreshore Road opposite the beach. At approximately one o`clock every Saturday afternoon, a hoard of children would nosily assemble opposite the main doors about three meters, from the theatre entrance. As soon as the usherettes opened the main doors, there was a unanimous roar of excitement as the children barged forward with their sixpence admission charge (two and a half pence, and nicknamed a 'tanner') clutched in their hands. After paying our tanner we would rush through the narrow passage way yelling excitedly into the main theatre to claim the best seats. After many arguments and scuffles, the lights were slowly dimmed; and then extinguished completely, amid great shouting and yells erupting around the darkened theatre, however all noise quickly subsided as the show began. Two cartoons were usually shown, followed perhaps by a short slapstick film featuring maybe the three Stooges or Laurel and Hardy, and then the lights would be switched back on for a small intermission. If you were lucky; and you had any money you could purchase a small tub of ice cream, chock bar (a chocolate covered ice cream bar) or a drink on a stick (ice lolly) from the usherette's laden tray, amid the bedlam of noise, talking, and arguing. Sometimes there could be some boys rolling in the aisles fighting. However, as soon as the lights dimmed there was a unanimous cheer once again as everybody settled back into their seats once more. Another short comedy film would be screened, and then, what everybody had been waiting for, from the previous week, the weekly serial. The serial, lasting about ten or fifteen minutes, and shown over about six to ten weekly episodes, consisted of perhaps Flash Gordon, Tarzan, or any one of the popular cowboy characters, such as Hopalong Cassidy or Roy Rogers. The ending of that days serial, had the hero in a very perilous position, but all would be revealed the following week   One particular serial that comes to my mind was 'Tex   Ritter and The Midnight Riders' Which always opened with a group of cowboys furiously ridding out from a darkened cave, wearing black klu kux clan type hoods. All of us were enthralled with the sight of the raiders and their black hoods, so much so that I pleaded with dad to make me a black hood as worn by the raiders. Worn down by my constant pleading dad relented, and taking an old black skirt belonging to mum he sewed up one end of the skirt and then he cut out two holes for the eyes and a wider hole for my mouth. Pleased with my appearance in the mirror, and picking up my cap firing pistol, I galloped out of the house slapping my bottom as though ridding a phantom horse, and out into the next street.   For no particle reason I knocked on Old Mrs Butlers front door. Mrs Butler was the local gossip, and Dad detested her.   As the door opened I aimed my cap firing gun at her and fired. Mrs Butler was so absolutely terrified of the sharp bang, followed by the hideous sight of a black hooded figure with a gun facing her, that she promptly fainted. A little while later all hell broke out, Mrs Butler stood on our doorstep ranting at mum about my escapade and threatening to call the police. When Dad got back home from work that evening, a flustered and angry mum retold the tale to him, and ordered that I should be punished for frightening Mrs Butler, Dads reply?

"Smacked! For causing that evil old wind bag to faint, he deserves a medal as big as a f----dustbin lid"

There were also three other cinemas in the town, however they were minor compared to the Odeon, and the Futurist.

Just a little away from the main street was the Capitol cinema which had no matinees or programs for children but catered mostly for the successful movies of the day. 'The Londesborough' had once been an old time music hall, however it had been converted into a cinema many years before, but it was demolished before I had reached my teenage years, but a few years earlier ,with my dad I did visit it a couple of times Even now I can still recall the dull gloomy entrance foyer, and the narrow double doors leading to the ground floor interior, also the dimly lit gas lights, and dirty cream painted walls of the narrow long winding staircase which led up to the balcony, looking down onto the ground floor and screen. The balcony known as the 'Gods ' had aisles of seats that rose so dramatically that sitting on the back rows you felt like a pilot of a spaceship. 'The Aberdeen' (later to be known as The Gaiety) was a far more pleasant and compact cinema, and for a short time it ran a fairly successful Saturday afternoon matinee. However, only a few years later it held a successful Sunday' Teenagers Night' which played a double bill of horror films, but it was the interval that became the main attraction, pop records of the day were played and the disc jockey always asked if it was a person's birthday that week, if so one of the records was given away as a present, Strangely my friends and I had numerous birthdays every month. Also in the interval a talent contest was held, in which a number of budding local pop groups first made their stage appearance

HI HO SILVER AWAY

Radio was still the most popular household media when I was a child, but television was fast becoming a desirable possession, but it was quite an expensive item. However dad and Mum were determined to have a television set, and

94

they both had been working hard to save for a deposit to buy one. Finally the day arrived for an Ariel to be fixed onto our chimney stack; and a television set to be installed. After school I, with Dave, Pete, and Sam, raced to my house with excitement. (Eric`s parents had already owned a television set for over a year) We all sat on the living room carpet in front of the cumbersome wooden cabinet in anticipation, just as dad arrived home from work. He switched the set on, and we all waited with bated breath for a picture to appear on the tiny screen. Suddenly a grainy black and white image appeared, and then the set fully opened up to the sight of a masked cowboy ridding a white horse, shouting

"Hi ho silver away."

From that moment on the television, or the telly as we were to call it, was to become a big part of our evening's entertainment. At the beginning the programs were mostly shown at teatime and early evenings and the programs were short, and the subjects limited. Very few of the major stars of the radio made the transaction to the small silver screen. Even to our young eyes many of the programs seemed very amateurish, but to supplement the British programs many programs were imported from America. The top American entertainment stars of the time, such as Perry Como, Lucile Ball, Phil Silvers, and George Burns, all had their own shows, while American crime shows such as Dragnet, Highway Patrol, and Sunset Strip, also were attracting a lot of attention. However, in abundance and filled with adventure and action were the popular Western series like Wagon Trail, Cheyenne, Gunsmoke, and Rawhide, which featured a young, tall slim, handsome actor by the name of Clint Eastwood. All the weekly Western series had a huge following not just the adults but also with the younger generation..

Football was without doubt the most played, and supported sport in Britain. However Scarborough, although having a well supported amateur side, had no lower division football teams of the F,A. within a two hour journey from the town,(never mind one of the major teams from the first division) so the only information we could gather was through the radio or the sport pages of the national papers, and the eagerly scanned photos in the weekly boys comics like the Hotspur, or the collectable cards in the packs of bubble gum, which had a famous international footballer on the front side of the card and on the back a snippet of information about the player. About two months after requiring the television set, along with dad and myself, five of my friends sat in our living room one Saturday afternoon and soaked up the atmosphere and revelled in the excitement of the 1958 F.A. cup final between Manchester United and Bolton Wanderers. Although regular weekly television football programs were not to appear until a decade later, the F.A. cup final was the sporting televised event of the year, and besides the match itself it was nearly a full afternoon of Soccer information. But very soon British television not only caught up with, but surpassed America, and over the years Britain has produced and made some world ground breaking programs. However I could reminisce endlessly and in detail over those programs, but even now after all those years ago, closing my eyes I can still see that grainy silver figure of a masked cowboy riding his white horse, and a voice crying a haughty "Hi ho silver away!"

CHAPTER 6

WE WISH YOU A MERRY CHRISTMAS

In our last year at Friarage Junior mixed School, we sat our eleven plus examinations to determine the academic level of our schooling for the next four years. Eric, always the most studious of us all, easily passed the examination, and after the summer holidays Eric was to start at The Scarborough High School for Boys. Dave, Pete, Sam, and I failed the examination so after the summer holidays we progressed from Friarage Junior mixed school to the Friarage Senior School for Boys. In the first term at the senior school about a month before the Christmas holidays, all the first-year boys took another written test; the results would determine what forms we would be attending after the Christmas holidays. Pete and I had done reasonably well, so our form was to be 1a, whereas Dave and Sam's form would be 1b. Those two exams, although not significant on their own, were actually the first step to the decline of our little gang. Eric was now attending a different school; Pete and I, after the Christmas holidays, would be in separate forms from Dave and Sam. Although we all still remained friends after school time, the gang was slowly disintegrating, as each one of us was to find new friends and different interests. That Christmas though was the defining change for us all from boys, into youths.

The spirit and goodwill of Christmas has now sadly faded. These days, months before the great event we are caught up in a relentless campaign by the media, supermarkets, and big business to engage in an orgy of materialistic indulgence. People fill up their shopping trolleys to the limit with enough food and drink to outlast a siege, and using credit cards to buy expensive presents that are not really needed or can be afforded, while at the same time scowling and complaining at the amount of money they are spending, and at the doleful task of writing and posting dozens of Christmas cards to people that they hardly know, or even care about. This is sad really, because Christmas should be the happiest and relaxed time of the year, it should be a bright light in a bleak season. Nowadays the gigantic early build-up to the event makes it a stressful expensive exercise, and in the process erasing what the significance of Christmas is all about, disregarding if you are religious or not. Perhaps I am looking through rose-coloured glasses now that I am much older, and I can only look back and see the good and happy times of my early life, yet I firmly believe that most of my life, and especially the early days of my life have been happy. However, even though times were still hard nearly sixty years ago, Christmas then was an unhurried magical and exciting time of the year, many things that we now take for granted were only but just a dream then, yet the aura, spirit, and goodwill of Christmas was all around to see and hear.

As the last two weeks before Christmas approached the regular lessons at school seemed to be less intent, and now that we had left the junior school there were no silly Christmas decorations to make, and no nativity scenes, but there were also no Christmas school party. Yet, even the teachers seemed to have an air of goodwill about them, all except for our own form master. Mr Butler, a fearsome ex-army sergeant, or Himmler as all the pupils called him. After lunch about a week before the school broke up for the Christmas holidays, the whole of the senior school assembled at St Thomas's church, (about a ten-minute walk from Friarage school) for the annual school Christmas carol service.

Each form sat together on the long rows of pews with their respective form master sitting at the end of the pews. After singing a communal carol, the white frocked vicar in a monotonous drawling voice droned on about the Christmas story. Bored, we sniggered, messed about, and generally fidgeted, much to Himmler's angry stares. More carols were then sung, but to liven up the dull afternoon some of us added our own lyrics to the carols, singing with gusto, such as,

"We three kings of Orient are, bearing gifts we travel so far. One on a scooter pressing the hooter. One in a scraggy old car, ooh---"

At the end of the service we said the Lord's Prayer, and I burst into helpless laughter when a fellow classmate changed the words to "Our father which farts in heaven, Harold be thy name." I received glaring, angry looks from Himmler, which guaranteed me a caning the following day.

The final day before the Christmas holidays, all lessons for that day were disbanded as the form masters played games or music, and organised fun quizzes with their respective forms. But no such luck for us. Himmler, for the entire morning lectured us on the importance of the signing of the Magna Carta, and how Oliver Cromwell changed the political and religious scene of England. To make matters worse for Pete and myself Himmler revealed the bad news that he was going to be the form master of 1a for the following year.

After dinner Himmler announced in a stern voice that there was to be a quiz, and to make sure everybody participated Himmler intended to ask each boy in turn a question. The questions as expected from Himmler were all of a serious nature, and any boy not answering his question correctly; received a severe tongue lashing from Himmler. Steve Grainger was a tall robust boy with a happy nature and a joker, and he feared no one, teachers included. After turning his wrath on some the first few boys' answers, Himmler, full of his own importance turned to Steve and snarled.

"Grainger. Who said, 'a horse, a horse, my kingdom for a horse'?"

Steve, a huge grin on his face replied.

"John Wayne sir."

All of us sniggered, but only slightly, for Himmler seething with rage bounded out of his chair, grabbed Steve roughly by his shirt collar, and dragging him to the front of the class held out his hand and whacked him hard with his ever-present cane. Steve, unperturbed just simply looked Himmler in the eye and grinned, before swaggering back to his desk.

Himmler, angry that his strict authority seemed to be undermined looked around for a safer easier target and on seeing Sam, Himmler snarled.

"Dawson! In which country is Delhi?"

Sam at first seemed perplexed, but then suddenly raising his arm and looking pleased with himself he answered confidently.

"He plays for Brazil sir,"

Again, the class sniggered at Sam`s unintentionally; but amusing innocent answer.

However, Himmler`s face turned a shade of purple. Unsure if Sam`s answer was a genuine mistake, or if Sam was carrying on this rebellious attitude he bawled.

"BE QUIET ALL OF YOU! "

Then turning back to Sam he growled.

"And you Dawson, I will overlook your stupidity this time; and I will ask you another question, so be sure to give me the correct answer this time. Now Dawson, as I explained the other day, the galaxy is made up of many stars and planets, Pluto is one of the furthest planets, now name the next two planets to Pluto."

Sam, cowering, but trying hard to understand the question, was completely baffled.

However, Himmler was impatient and determined to reassert his authority, he struck his desk with his cane and snarled angrily.

"Well Dawson, you thick head, answer the question boy."

Suddenly a realisation came over Sam`s face, and lifting his arm high in the air he blurted excitedly,

"Sir, sir, I know the next two It`s Mickey Mouse and Donald Duck."

The whole class erupted into howls of laughter except for Himmler, who, shooting out of his chair went completely berserk, grabbing a bewildered Sam by his ear, he dragged him out to the front of the class, and holding Sam's arm out he whacked him two times across the palm of his hand. Himmler, his eyes glazed, and frothing at the mouth, stared hard at Sam, and expecting an unconditional apology from Sam he bellowed.

"Well Dawson, what do you to say to me?"

Sam, tears welling up in his eyes looked pitifully up at Himmler and replied, "Merry Christmas Sir."

That Christmas Ted was living and working in London, Francis was spending her second Christmas in Cottingham Sanatorium, Teresa, who by now had three children, was living in Germany with her soldier husband Arthur, so that just left mum dad, and me at home to celebrate Christmas. With just over a week to go before the big event, Christmas preparations at home began to slowly move into place. Two cardboard boxes containing the previous year's Christmas decorations, and a small green adjustable artificial

Christmas tree were removed from the top of mum and dad's wardrobe. That sacred shrine the front room, usually reserved only for important visitors or special occasions, was opened up and was revealed in all its polished glory. Mum carefully cleaned and dusted the decorations, while dad and I with specific instructions from mum, hung up the decorations in the front room. The cumbersome mahogany table situated directly under the bay window became the focal point of the room. The Christmas tree in a silver foiled covered pot was placed directly in the centre of the table with strands of silver tinsel intertwined through its green plastic branches, and an assortment of small coloured glass bulbs dangling gracefully on the branches (electric bulbs were at the time unheard of in our vicinity). On top of the tree dad had fastened a large silver star, and at each side of the tree mum placed Christmas religious figurines and models of the Nativity. Only the Christmas cards sent by close friends and relations were allowed to be displayed on the mantelpiece of the highly polished pine surround of the tiled fireplace, the rest of the cards were pinned on to a cotton line held by drawing pins across the chimney breast. To complete the decorations a few sprigs of holly were laid on the inside of the bay window sill, and two small sprigs of the holly were taped onto the top corners of the large sitting room mirror, along with small balls of cotton wool, then on mum's strict instructions the front room was closed and out of bounds until Christmas Eve.

Early January, when the insurance man made his weekly call, mum would begin her new Christmas club account. Each week mum would regularly pay along with her and dad's insurance money, a small amount of money into the Christmas account. The Christmas club money was then withdrawn a couple of weeks before Christmas, this provided us with all the extras. There was no fridge or freezer, just a small larder, so most of the food would be purchased fresh a couple of days before Christmas Day. Also a few weeks before Christmas Dad would call in at the off licence in the next street, to purchase bottles of pale ale, milk stout , lemonade, ginger ale , and as a special a treat for mum a bottle of Harvey's Bristol Cream Sherry.

Although the myth of Father Christmas had been exposed some years previous, this did not deter Dave, Pete Eric, Sam and myself, from visiting Santa's Grotto situated in the basement of Boyes Store in Queen Street. The admission was free, however at the entrance to the grotto stood a young woman dressed as a fairy, if you purchased a shilling ticket (five pence) from her before you entered, at the other end of the grotto stood another fairy and if you produced your ticket you were allowed a dip for a wrapped present from one of the two large barrels, pink for the girls and blue for the boys. Every year in the grotto there was a display with imaginative scenes of Christmas, with models of elves in Santa's workshop making toys, or loading up his sleigh. At the end of the glittering grotto Father Christmas was seated on a large leather chair, resplendent in his long white beard, and wearing a red hat and gown trimmed with white fur. Santa listened attentively as smaller boys and girls, sitting on his knee, whispered into his ear of their ideal Christmas presents. Although the rest of us looked at the grotto as just a seasonal spectacular, Sam, his one lens spectacles reflecting the sparkling colours, walked slowly through the grotto completely memorised at the brightly coloured scenes, he then stood in awe at the sight of Santa resplendent in his chair. Although we teased him, and he denied it, Sam still believed in Father Christmas, or was it perhaps a joyful mesmerizing distraction from his usual every day brutal world of poverty?

We rarely visited the town centre through the year unless taken there by our mums for new clothes. But at Christmas the town centre drew us like a magnet. The aura of Christmas and the season of goodwill was everywhere, captivated by the happy faces of the crowded shoppers. Outside Johnsons the butchers, on Aberdeen Walk, rows of unplucked geese, turkeys, and chickens, dangled from large hooks fastened onto a long metal rail above the shop windows. Displayed in one window were trays of ducks, turkeys and chickens, plucked and headless all ready for the oven, while in the other window different sizes of pork pies, and sausage rolls vied for space with mixed joints of meat, and trays of bacon. Inside the shop itself a thick solid wooden table was laden with trays of eggs, while behind the counter the plump red-faced Mr Johnson and his assistants in their blue and white stripped aprons, laughed and cajoled with the smiling customers while cutting up, or serving joints of meat and poultry.

'Quartons' fruit and vegetable shops, always popular throughout the year, were bustling the final two days before the big event. Apart from the usual fruit and vegetables, also crammed in their open sacks or wooden boxes, the seasonal delicacies of nuts still in their shells in open sacks were on display. On the back shelf standing like a line of guardsmen stood little wooden boxes of exotic dates with the tempting title 'Eat Me'. On the lower shelves were bunches of green and red grapes they looked delicious and inviting, yet to us, as unobtainable as a stroll on the moon.

All the shops held their own fascinations but without doubt Elliot's toy shop on Castle Road was our favourite. With our noses pressed hard against the two large windows we stared in awe at the Aladdin's cave of toys. In one window, strictly for the girls, dolls of all sizes, complete with dummy's and feeding bottles, nestled between sheets of stiff coloured cardboard containing a junior hairdressing set, or a complete tea set containing cups and saucers, plates, knife forks and spoons, all in red plastic, and a nurse's hat and uniform lay amongst the many other girlie interests, However, it was the other window for boys that held our fascination. The entire top shelf was dedicated to the armed forces and their weapons of war, plastic toy soldiers ran knelt or lay, with the obligatory rifle, machine gun, or flame thrower in their hand. While toy tanks and artillery guns, nestled between scaled down German and English fighter aeroplanes. The shelf below featured the Wild West. Toy cowboys and Indian figures, covered wagons, rubber tomahawks and knifes, cap firing rifles, hand guns, and cowboy hats. The bottom of the window was more for the pacifist kind of boy, a self-making pottery set, complete with rubber moulds and mixing powder. An assortment of toy motor boats, aircraft self-assembly kits, a bus conductor's cap and ticket machine, and hoards of miniature cars vans and lorries. We spent a lot of time arguing between ourselves which of the toys belonged to whom.

Carol singing could be a lucrative way of making a little money in the dark cold evenings before Christmas. That Christmas was like a well organised military exercise as the five of us agreed on a battle plan. The Avenues are a row of streets running off Dean Road, we decided that each of us would take an Avenue apiece and then we were to meet up at the top of Dean Road to pool our money. But Pete argued that Sam, because of his appearance would make very little money so he should only get a smaller share, and to my annoyance Dave, who lately was becoming very obnoxious and argumentative, agreed with Pete, but after some strong words from Eric and myself, Pete and Dave reluctantly agreed to the original plan. Usually any ventures meant two, or all of us doing it together, but on this occasion each of us were on our own. The response I received varied with each house. After Knocking on the door and then singing a carol, in some houses there was no reply, at other houses after only singing a few lines of a carol the door quickly opened, a few coins were thrust into my hand and before I could finish, the door closed again. However, some people stood on their door steps, arms folded, and demanded one or two more carols, making sure my money was well earned. After about two very cold hours we all met at the top of Dean Road, with Dave laughing and scoffing at Sam's absence. However, on reaching the very top of Dean Road there was Sam, sat on a garden wall looking pleased with himself. As we began to empty the coins out of our pockets onto the pavement Dave began angrily pointing at Sam accusing him for not making any money, and once again arguing that as such Sam should not have a share of our earnings. However. after Sam emptied his own two bulging pockets onto the pavement, we stared in disbelief at the amount Sam had collected, which was nearly half again as what the four of us together had collected. Sam then modestly explained how he had collected so much money. Sam had taken note from singing on the coaches in the summer, how his appearance and voice gave him an advantage, so, with it being Christmas he thought that people would be more sympathetic than usual. Sam also reasoned that if he only sang "We wish you a merry Christmas" the shortest seasonal greeting he would be able to cover more houses in less time, and so collect more money. From that night; although at the time I wasn`t aware, it was the steady decline of our gang, and especially my own close friendship with Dave. Also, I began to realise that Sam was not the actual slow dimwit that everybody thought he was, and allowing for his lack of education, Sam did indeed have a very sharp business brain.

Every other working day dad and mum rose early. Dad, who had now started his own window cleaning business, before his breakfast cleaned out the fireplace, and then he lit the coal fire, while Mum busied herself with the breakfast and other household chores, before going on to her morning employment as a cleaner for a local furniture store. But on Christmas Eve morning they were both up and about even earlier, because Christmas Eve day was the busiest day of the year, especially for mum, because it was one endless round of cleaning, baking and preparing, along with numerous trips to the shops, yet mum seemed to enjoy and even thrive on all the hard work.

Every other night, to mum's annoyance, I would gulp down my tea before rushing out to join my mates, but Christmas Eve was definitely a time to stay indoors. That night the house was alive with the sights and smells of Christmas. In the kitchen the Christmas pudding, wrapped in a muslin cloth, which had been prepared some weeks previously, had been removed from the larder and placed onto the kitchen table. Mum filled the house with the mouth-watering aroma of mince pies, sausage rolls, and other pastries, all fresh and hot from the oven. Meanwhile, in the freezing, dark back yard, dad was seated on a wooden chair, a woodbine in his mouth, plucking an enormous goose, with the kitchen door open for some light, white feathers scattering around him like a fall of snow. After removing the giblets, he washed and cleaned the goose and then he placed it onto a large platter, ready and waiting for the oven the following morning. Dad then began to take out the bottles he had purchased from the off licence from the cupboard beneath the stairs. As I carried the bottles into the front room dad lined them up on the top of the sideboard like a squad of soldiers. Meanwhile mum had placed a plastic tray on to the sideboard and filled it with glasses and a bottle opener, she then brought in a bowl of fresh fruit and a big bowl of unshelled nuts, and a nutcracker, and laid them carefully onto the coffee table. Mum, after rearranging the sideboard and coffee table several times, making sure that everything was to her satisfaction, finally declared the front room open, but with a dire warning, directed at me in particularly, to keep the room clean and tidy. Eventually when all the preparations for the following day had been completed, dad unplugged the huge television set in the living room, and with great difficulty he carried the heavy cumbersome set into the front room. The front room coal fire had now been burning brightly for a few hours, and alongside all the decorations it gave the room a warm and cosy glow. Mum, her chores now completed for the day, sat down next to dad on the settee with a well-earned glass of milk stout, while dad, a glass of beer in one hand and a woodbine smouldering between his fingers in his other hand, switched on the television set, (although it would take many minutes for a picture and sound to appear). The set was encased in a large polished cabinet with a 14inch screen (350mm), and it produced a grainy black and white picture, however to us it was a modern day miracle, for It was like having a mini cinema in your own home. Even though the programmes were poor, and the broadcasting closed down early in the evening, what did I care as I lay on the front room carpet, legs waving in the air, reading with glee, Biffo the Bear, and Desperate Dan's Christmas capers in that week's Christmas edition of the Beano and Dandy comics, while eating a warm mince pie and drinking ginger beer. Mum and dad watched a Christmas choir broadcast from a

London church. But what really occupied my mind that night was the excitement and thought of Christmas Day.

Mum and dad in the early years could not afford Christmas presents for each other, and when they left school Teresa, Francis and Ted, received no more Christmas presents from mum and dad either. Visiting Francis, who had contacted T.B and was in the Sanatorium in Cottingham, so every Sunday through the year was a four hour round trip by bus, and taking necessities and small luxuries for Francis, drained mum and dad's already tight budget, so I knew that any presents for me would be minimal. However, unbeknown to myself, mum and dad had been putting a little money aside for me for that Christmas morning. Oh! how well I remember the excitement of seeing a toy replica German luger pistol complete with three boxes of caps (inserted in the gun to make a banging sensation), an Eagle comic book annual, and a smoker's set, comprising of a pipe made of liquorice, a packet of candy cigarettes with the tips stained red, and a small fat cream filled chocolate cigar with a gold band around its centre, (this was before the evils of smoking were really known) and a Cadburys selection box, all laying, but without wrapping paper, on the front room settee. Though by today's standard those gifts might seem miserly, mum and dad had worked hard to provide me with those few presents, and to me they were prized possessions. Although I can't remember in precise detail everything that happened that morning, I do recall getting a smack on the back of my head from dad for firing the gun in the house so early in the morning. I also remember going out later that morning to meet up with the gang on William Street, and seeing Mozart's fat black cat fast asleep on the front garden wall. Creeping stealthy close to the cat I fired three shots rapidly with my new luger pistol, the cat shot up, yelped, bolted across the road, and scaled three garden walls in succession like a thoroughbred racehorse, before disappearing from view. (Now, I feel ashamed of this prank)

There was total excitement on the buildings that morning. Dave and Pete both had replica cowboy plastic rifles complete with rolls of caps. Eric had a Dan Dare space gun, that when the trigger was squeezed it lighted up in green and red and made whirring sounds, but poor Sam only had a sorry looking rubber tomahawk which he stuck in the waistband of his patched-up shorts. That morning many skirmishes were fought on the battle fields of Europe, and on the planets of Mars and Jupiter, and over the open Kansas plains many Indians were defeated or taken prisoner. However poor Sam was totally inadequate with his rubber tomahawk; alas he took no prisoners and he never killed anyone, yet he himself was captured repeatedly, and died many times over.

There were no Christmas crackers to pull, no exotic wines to drink, and no prawn cocktail for a starter, but in abundance for Christmas dinner there was plenty of good fresh food, seasonal vegetables, roast and mash potatoes, Yorkshire puddings, stuffing, and at the centre piece of the feast, the roast goose, with the Christmas pudding being the stomach filling grand finally.

Much to my annoyance I was not allowed out to play out for the rest of the day. But full to bursting point I did not really complain as I sat on the carpet and read my Eagle annual. After dinner, but before washing the pots mum, a glass of sherry in her hand sat down to listen to the Queens speech on the radio in the living room. Although she could watch it on the television, mum always the traditionalist chose the radio, however, dad a staunch republican, preferred not to listen, and moved into the front room where dad and I watched the Bertram Mills circus on the television. After the Queens speech mum faced the awesome task of washing and cleaning up, and after she began to make hordes of sandwiches, and cutting up the large pork pie and sausage rolls. She then placed them onto four large separate plates alongside jars of pickled onions, beetroot, and piccalilli, and covered all of them up with tea towels, before settling down with dad and I in the front room

Early Christmas day evening, close friends whom mum and dad had invited, with Dave and his family among them began to arrive. When I look back, I am totally amazed at how such a small living room and front room, with over a dozen people milling about could possibly not feel crowded, if it did nobody complained

Dad handed out bottles of pale ale to the men, and bottles of Stout to the women, while mum brought in the piled-up plates of sandwiches, pork pie, and sausage rolls, accompanied by a range of pickles, As everybody began to relax humorous everyday stories and happenings were retold, amid howls of giggling and loud laughter. Suddenly dad broke wind, mum, quite tipsy by now, and trying hard not to laugh, clutched tightly to her glass of sherry she cried out half-heartedly.

"Oh Eddie, stop that"

Dad, always the comedian, got down on his hands and knees and pretending to look under the settee replied,

"Well I would if I could find which way the b----- thing went."

Mum, putting down her sherry with one hand while trying to cover her mouth with her other hand, and along with the rest of the company burst into uncontrolled laughter, and none more so than Dave's dad Charlie, a huge, kindly man with a loud thunderous voice. All that night Dave, his younger brother, and I, sat silently, totally absorbed in the conversations and laughter, drinking our lemonade and ginger beer while eating the home-made food. As the evening wore on dad brought out his mouth organ and everybody joined in an improvised medley of songs. Mum had a very lilting singing voice, which unfortunately she hardly used, but that Christmas night when mum sang with a smile on her face, everybody listened in silent admiration, and I became very aware for the first time of all the hard work and sacrifices that she and dad had made over the years to feed and clothe their family, and the struggles just to keep their own heads above water. Yet they, with all their friends and neighbours never complained or moaned of their lot. Much later that same night, as I lay snuggled up in bed with my precious luger pistol close to me, listening to the continuous sound of the laughter and singing downstairs, I once again pictured the rare sight of mum smiling, and with dad, relaxing and singing along with their friends, while thinking to myself, why life could not be like this all the time, laughing and singing, with no cares or worries, and every day being just one long Christmas day.

Left: The author Terry, when a schoolboy

Below: Irena and Terry on their wedding day with his mother and father (left) and Irena's father (right)).

Above: Terry in Gibraltar on a building site.

Below: With his two daughters Joanna and Sharon

114

Terry and Irena with their three grandchildren, Nicole, Jamie and Kirstin.

CHAPTER 7

DON'T SPARE THE CANE.

Friarage Senior School for Boys meant just that, because in Scarborough at that particular time, when you were 11 years old and reaching senior level; and after leaving a mixed boys' and girls' junior school, the sexes were kept apart. In our area the girls went to either The Convent or Central School, and the boys attended the senior Friarage School. The teachers at Friarage seniors were in the main strict but fair, although the odd ones were downright sadistic. However now when I look back, apart from the quiet or submissive pupils the rest of the school intakes certainly needed a firm hand. A lot of the teachers had been through, and had survived the war, which I now fully appreciate, for they must have seen a lot of suffering and horrendous sights, so this perhaps accounted somewhat for their frustration, and at times angry moods when they were trying hard to prepare and educate the next generation. Although this same excuse could not be said for the school dentist whom I am certain enjoyed the pain and terror he inflicted on his captive chair bound victims. Dressed in a starched long white gown, with his close cropped hair and gold rimmed glasses, with an evil grin spread across his fat face, he looked and acted like a typical Nazi officer. Thankfully I only ever had one tooth extracted, but I still can recall in horror as he roughly pressed the black rubber mask onto my face and the terrible smelling gas entered my mouth and nostrils. As the chair slowly reclined, the dreaded electric drill stared down on me like a hideous torture instrument, and near to suffocation I thankfully drifted into a deep sleep. Later, still drowsy I staggered back into the waiting room, where even tough boys were perched on the edge of their chairs and looking up at me in horror, like turkeys waiting for the Christmas slaughter.

As I have already explained our gang had now splintered after a mid-term test, so Pete and myself were now in class 1a, commanded by the aggressive and sadistic form master Mr Butler or better known to the pupils as 'Himmler'.

Friarage County Modern was not the only senior school in the catchment area, St Peter's Catholic school was in close proximity, but Friarage was the only church of England senior boys' school, so apart from those other boys who with ourselves had moved up from the Friarage junior school, new boys from the Northstead Junior mixed School amalgamated with us, so new friends were found, or in some cases new enemies were made. In the main the boys from Northstead junior school and the boys from Friarage junior school mixed reasonably well; however, we all seemed to keep within our own known circles. Pete and myself drifted into a loose gang of about six other boys from the bottom end, I had always been quite overweight, however I could look after myself so after the first initial skirmishes with the new intakes we all settled in well. In our first year at Friarage, all those boys fortunate to have a bike were expected to take a cycle proficiency test. One morning every week for a about month, we rode our bikes onto a section of tarmacked area above the OpenAir theatre, where a Police Sergeant taught us to ride safely on a chalked out piece of road, equipped with road signs. He then lectured us on the rules and safety of taking a bike out onto the open road. On the final day a road test was to take place, but while the Sergeant was giving instructions of the forth coming test, some of my friends and I began fooling about. Suddenly the Sergeant, who was standing some distance away, pointed at me and bellowed.

"YOU! The boy with the blue jumper ride quickly towards me, now."

I was puzzled at his order, however, I drove at some speed towards him, when suddenly holding up his hand the sergeant stepped out in front of me, and without stopping, I rode over his foot. The sergeant, after limping about, screamed abuse at me and shouted that that the object of the test was to test our braking skills, the following week all the boys received their cycle proficiency certificates, that is, except myself. Punishment from the teachers was nearly an everyday occurrence for some of us, and certain teachers had their own idea of corporal punishment. Mr Green the metal work teacher used a leather strap which he kept locked up in his desk. Though he used the strap sparingly, if you ever had been at the receiving end of one of Mr Green's punishments then in future you always gave metal work a lot more care and attention. Mr Merriweather the P.E. master who always seemed to be permanently dressed in a dark blue track suit, and wearing plimsolls (an early day version of trainers), had his own form of punishment. If, while in the gym a boy had displeased Mr Merriweather, the culprit was asked:

'What size plimsolls do you wear boy?'

After the boy had declared his shoe size Mr Meriwether with a smile on his face would ask the boy to bring a plimsoll from a rack in the gym, but, two sizes bigger than the boy's size, he would then order the boy to bend over and smack his backside with the plimsole (we would be wearing only thin nylon shorts so the pain was intense) which made the boy straighten up sharply. Mr Merriweather would then hollow loudly,

118

"Did I tell you to move boy? No I didn't! Well bend over again then."

And smirking, he would once more repeat the punishment. Needless to say those of us who could stand the pain, remained bent down in future

A fact that always seems to be common with some of my generation is that the school meals were seen as horrid and boring, but compared to today's processed junk food; the school meals were well balanced and nutritious, besides which, I was told by my parents to always be grateful for whatever food I was given, because unlike a lot of children in the world I was fortunate to have the choice, a saying that is sadly still relevant in today's world. The dining hall, was situated about twenty metres from the school in St Sepulchre Street. The hall consisted of rows of large trestle tables and long forms to sit on suitable for seating about ten boys to each table. Large jugs of water were placed in the middle of the table, and a plastic beaker and a set of cutlery laid out for each boy. There were two courses (each day was different) a main meal and a pudding, which were brought to the tables by the school prefects. The main meal would consist of perhaps a stew, a meat pie, or sliced cooked meat, served with potatoes, two vegetables, and gravy. However, in the summer months a series of salads were served. The puddings were either rice, sago, tapioca, jam sponge, and my favourite, corn flake pie, which consisted of corn flakes stuck to a pastry base by a thick layer of treacle and covered with custard.

Football was undoubtedly the preferred sport for most boys, including myself, but unfortunately because of my weight problem, speed was not my forte, but I was always accepted in any football games in or out of school times. Mornings, break times, and dinner times, in fact every day in the school yard, a game of football would be in play.

119

There could be sometimes a dozen or more to each side, using only a tennis ball. One afternoon a week we would be taken by a coach to the town's schools playing fields, situated on Oliver mount, overseen by Mr Merriweather the sports master. We would strip down to our vest, and P.E. shorts, in the dilapidated changing rooms. Out on the playing fields we would be given P.E. lessons, even in the foulest of weather. After a bout of P.E. we would then put on our football boots ready for a game of football. Two sides would be selected, boys who were either not interested in football, or not good enough, would be ordered to remain as spectators. Mr Merriweather was in his element both as the referee, and acting as a England International for both sides, screaming and hollering for the ball, while barging around the field like a rampant bull. One very wet and murky afternoon Mr Merriweather was galloping down the touchline at great speed, with the ball at his feet, knocking aside any boy who stood in his way. Looking up he screamed hysterically for myself and another boy to run into the opposition's goal area, where Mr Merriweather had kicked the ball. Both the other boy and I looked up in awe as the ball dropped down like a huge stone. The leather ball was very cumbersome and heavy even in very dry weather, but on a wet, mud soaking surface like that day, the football became a lethal, giant cannon ball. As the ball descended down towards us Mr Merriweather screamed hysterically, "Well Head it then one of you two idiots."

I, after muttering a few coarse words under my breath, ignored his order and stepped aside, however even though the other boy was also petrified, he closed his eyes and jumped a few feet up in the air; just as the ball, with a loud thud connected to the crown of his head. The boys head seemed to disappear into his neck, as he fell down on the mud sodden field, while the loose leather laces of the ball whipped his cheeks, before bouncing over the bye line and out of play. I, along with the rest of the boys laughed loudly at the boy, who was now laid on the ground groaning and holding his head. Mr Merewether however, furious that his precision like pass had been squandered, picked up the ball, strode angrily up to me, and snarled

"So, you think its funny do you White, well see if this will make you laugh, you imbecile?"

And he furiously hurled the sodden cannon ball at my face. The invention of the 'Frido' ball was a revelation for football games. 'The Frido' was a red plastic ball, in size; equivalent to a real football, and we played with the Frido on waste grounds and fields. They were cheap to buy, but more importantly it was only a fraction in weight of the real leather cased football, and stayed the same weight in all weathers, which really mattered when heading the ball, The only downside being; that in extremely windy weather, the ball when kicked to the air hung like a gliding bird, or alternatively, if kicked into the oppositions half, with the wind against you, the ball, would return back into your own half.

The teachers; like the lessons were varied. Each class had its own form master, who also specialised in certain subjects. Himmler was not only our form master and English teacher but sometimes he was our geography teacher. It was rumoured that Himmler had spent some considerable time in India, so if he could be persuaded to talk about his India experiences then some precious time from boring lessons could be saved. However, Himmler was not only a strict disciplinarian but he was also acute to scheming pupils. A number of times somebody had carefully orchestrated Himmler to wax lyrically about his adoring India, just to make the lesson go faster, but after a while he would return back to the lesson. Yet one morning it all went wrong. Having spent twenty minutes describing in depth the habits and occupations of the Indian people, Himmler decided to return back to his English lesson, but Steve Grainger who was seated next to me, wanted to waste more time, so thrusting up his hand up he asked,

"Sir, why do the people in India have brown skins, and Africans have black skins?"

Himmler glowered, and snarled back,

"It's simple Grainger, it's a pigment of the skin."

Steve smirking, replied,

"What's a pig skin got to do with it sir?"

For a few seconds there was some sniggering, as Himmler's eyes rolled, and then frothing at the mouth, he suddenly grabbed his cane and rushed at Steve. Dragging him to the front of the class Himmler ordered Steve to hold out his hand before whacking it hard three times. Steve however, unperturbed, walked back to his desk still smirking. Fuming, Himmler looked around at the rest of the class for vengeance, he saw me smiling, pounced on me, and dragged me to the front of the class, and he gave me the same punishment as Steve. Sadistic? No, just totally insane. There were many so called scams to take away the pain of the cane, rub your hands with chalk, spit on them before the punishment, pull away your hand at the last minute (I tried this once and the cane whacked my fingertips, resulting in more agony) But alas nothing dulled the actual pain.

The Headmaster, and sometimes our English teacher, was Mr Davis, known affectionately to the pupils as Dizzy. However, Mr Davis was far from dizzy, in fact he was a very well educated and intelligent teacher, but unfortunately although he wore very thick spectacles, he was still very short sighted. Dizzy was a hard task master, but unlike some of the other teachers he was well liked by the pupils, but because of his short sightedness we played many pranks on him. The English lessons were sometimes conducted in the school library which doubled up as a classroom. Dizzy would set a subject for the lesson, and then order the class to write about the subject. Then he would return back to his desk, and with his nose nearly touching the books or papers he had stacked up in front of himself, he would begin to mark them. If a pupil asked a question he would look up impatiently from his marking, point to a set of six large encyclopaedias on a shelf and say,

"You will find any answer that you require in those encyclopaedias over there, so just use you're your eyes and look."

One day Pete and I gathered up all the encyclopaedias and silently crept up to Alan Simpson the class swot, who as usual was engrossed heavily in his work. We silently placed the encyclopaedias onto an empty chair besides him, and then Pete walked up to Dizzy, and asked him a question. Dizzy looked up angrily at Pete, and pointed to the now empty shelf, while giving his stock reply.

"Harrison, you should know by now that the answer that you require can be found in one of those encyclopaedias, if you only just open your eyes and look."

Pete, with a straight face, replied.

"I would sir, only Alan Simpson has taken them all."

Dizzy squinted hard at Alan Simpson, and seeing all the encyclopaedias piled beside him, Dizzy roared at him angrily. At the mention of his name Alan Simpson`s head sprung up. By now Dizzy was in a foul mood, and ordered Alan to come up to his desk, where Dizzy gave him a verbal onslaught. Alan, an undoubted teacher's pet, and usually at the centre for praise rather than abuse, to the delight of the rest of the class, burst into tears. Mr Pilgrim taught at Friarage for only about one year, but he made his mark on the class, and certainly on myself. Mr Pilgrim was the math's teacher, and he was a very heavy smoker, identified by his heavily nicotine stained fingers, bad breath, and his smoke ridden clothes, but he also possessed a vile temper. One day while marking our previous math's lesson, he called out my name, and demanded that I approach his desk. Puzzled, I obeyed his order and stood looking at him. Slowly he looked up at me and snarled.

"White, I have just been marking your math's book from last week, and on one of the answers you have written pounds instead of potatoes."

Pausing, then putting his foul-smelling face close to mine he snarled,

"Don`t you know the difference between pounds and potatoes White?

Smiling, I replied,

"Yes sir you can eat potatoes."

Suddenly without warning Mr Pilgrim roared, and jumping up from his chair he began to violently smack me about my head with his open hands, and although the smacks hurt me, the smell of his putrid breath, and his nicotine smelling clothes, were even more nauseating.

Mr Allison, christened by the pupils as 'Sawdust head' was the woodwork and technical drawing teacher, who rarely smiled or joked, and he taught his lessons very seriously indeed, so much so that some of the pupils were actually terrified at the approach of one of his lessons. 'Sawdust head' always wore a brown overall over his smartly pressed clothes and gave his instructions in a threatening snarl. He never gave praise to any boy, even though the boy might be gifted in the art of woodwork. But a boy who might lack practical ability would be subjected to his foul outburst of indignation and scorn. His preferred method of punishment? Anything that came at hand. It was not unknown for 'Sawdust Head' to lash out in a temper and throw any item of wood that he might be holding in his hand at the time. It was rumoured that he once hurled a wood chisel across three work benches just missing a boy's head by a matter of inches.

It may seem that all the teachers were sadistic bullies, who could only gain any sort of order or respect from their charges by using abusive language, scorn, and a variety of corporal punishments. However, this was far from the norm, because the majority of the teachers were strict but fair, and some even commanded a huge respect from the pupils, without a raised voice or the use of violence. Mr Appleton was for a short time our Geography teacher, he was a slim tall man, who during the course of the war had seen a lot of action in the battlefields of Europe. He spoke in a clear precise voice, as he described the habitants and the terrain of the countries around the world. Occasionally, when asked, Mr Appleton would give honest and graphic details of the horrors of the war through his now converted pacifist's eyes. Needless to say, Mr Appleton's lessons were always an anticipated event, and he was listened too in a respectful silence. Mr Wiltshire, was a relief history teacher for two terms, but in his appearance, he was the complete opposite to Mr Appleton. Rosy cheeked, short and stout, Mr Wiltshire spoke with a loud Yorkshire accent. Yet he made characters and events in his lessons seem so alive, and he coloured our education when he described his spell-binding, but harsh childhood, on a small hill farm high up in the Yorkshire Dales. It may seem pure coincidence but my history and geography yearly exam marks that year, were very high. There were many hilarious situations by the pupils, and comic reactions by the various teachers that I can recall, but I only wanted to outline my senior school years. It may seem that our school days were an endless parade of scams, pranks, and punishments. But in reality, we worked hard in our lessons, and for the most part we were respectful pupils, and we received by today's standard, a strong grounding in general education. Dyslexia was unknown at the time, so anybody with learning difficulties was unfortunately regarded as backward. However, unlike today, a large majority of pupils left school with the basic grounding in reading and writing, and with the knowledge of the world around them. As for the corporal punishment, yes, a few of the teachers were spiteful and cruel, but the majority were fair and excellent teachers, and besides; there is no doubt we did deserve the punishment, but it left no psychological or mental damage to anybody, just a sore hand or backside, and perhaps a bruised ego. Smoking in public was then considered normal for both male and females alike, but only when reaching the age of sixteen, and after all, didn't all the big television and movie stars of the day hold the obligatory cigarette in their hand or mouth, which made it fashionable? A number of my friends, me included, had taken up this adult pastime while at school, but of course out of sight of any adults, especially teachers, where an instant caning was assured. At most newsagents, cigarettes could be purchased without any questions, and there were many brands, and some cigarettes could even be bought in packets of fives. The outside school toilets were a favourite venue and hideaway, as the smoke would drift away in the open air. At break times the toilets were heavily used, but not for their intended purpose. The health hazards of tobacco were then relatively unknown, so was it any wonder that most boys left school addicted to the evils of tobacco. Thankfully I gave up smoking when I was thirty years of age.

CHAPTER 8

AND OF THOSE DAYS

I think it was George Bernard Shaw who said `Youth is wasted on the young', but I would strongly disagree, for when you are young you view everything in black and white; you take everybody and everything on face value, there is no danger in what you do, today is for living, tomorrow takes care of itself. You look on life as a game, a challenge. Things that you did or said when you were younger, you shake your head in disbelief when you are older, or is it because you have now conformed, and been shaped in to what society expects of you? When you are young you are dancing to a world that is flying, the days are never long enough, yet tomorrow seems so far away. Leaving Junior school can be a daunting experience for some children, because before joining the Senior school there were no cautions, or thoughts to the future, yet now in the Senior school the world seemed to be a hard task master, full of rules and regulations, yet that same world could light and colour your life in the years to come, so many changes, so many paths to take, so many decisions to make. That first Christmas at senior level was a defining time for all of us even though there was no intentional plan, just an awareness that things were changing and we all seemed to be changing too in our own individual ways.

Dave and I had been close friends for a long time, and we had done almost everything together. Yet when we moved to the senior school Dave changed, he became remorse and surly, becoming involved in fights, alienating all the other boys against him, including Pete, Eric and Sam. Having been close friends with each other I tried to reason with Dave, I wanted to make him see sense, and to realise that because of his attitude he was isolating himself, but Dave became abusive and we ended up parting on bad terms. From then on we all ignored Dave completely. About a year before we were due to leave school Dave, alongside his parents and his older brother, emigrated to Canada. Now as I look back, perhaps with hindsight I should have tried harder to understand the reason for his attitude, I wish we could have parted on good terms, but unfortunately that was never to be. I never saw or heard of Dave again.

Eric though never changed, he was always the happy dependable one. However it was inevitable that he would drift away, because attending the High school meant a lot of studying for Eric. Also our favourite sport Football, was replaced for Eric by rugby, a sport much more suited to Eric's build and strength. Weekends for Eric meant if not studying or working in his Fathers shop, he would take bike rides into the country with his new friends or indulge himself with model making, which held no interests to the rest of us, so Eric, although still friendly, had now found new mates and hobbies. When Eric left school he studied to be an architect, and he drifted even more from our environment. Then in his early twenties Eric married and moved away from Scarborough, I would like to think that wherever he is now Eric still remembers those distant, care free days.

Pete, like Dave, changed when we began at Senior school but for the better. No more the worrier, the moaner, the mother's boy. Pete blossomed, and instead of being led, he became the leader, strong and decisive. Although on leaving school Pete went from one menial employment to another, for it seemed as though he was searching for something in life but had not yet found what he wanted.

Two years after leaving school Pete also moved away from Scarborough to Sheffield, with his mother who had remarried. A few years later I learnt that Pete had joined the Army, and he had found the carefree and adventurous life that he had been searching for. In the late sixties when the troubles erupted in Northern Ireland Pete was among the first of the British peace keeping force to be sent over to Northern Ireland. It was in the mid-seventies when I heard from a school friend that Pete, now a corporal and heading towards a distinguished career. But a few months later, on his second tour of duty in the province, Pete was killed in an I.R.A. ambush. At the time I was only in my twenties, and although I had experienced the death of older people, including my own father, Pete's untimely death came as a great shock to me. However, death was to enter my life a number of times in my later years, and one death in particular was to bring a great change to me in many ways.

Sam, the boy with the hand me down clothes, and the drunken sadistic Father, left school with very little education. Although Sam and I both lived in the same town, after leaving school our paths rarely crossed. Sam began his own milk round, and a few years later he was involved in a number of business ventures. Fifteen years later Sam was an acute and successful business and property man, married with a family, and on his way to being very rich. Dyslexia was unknown at the time, but I am convinced that Sam was a victim of that illness, however like most suffers of dyslexia he excelled at other aspects in life, which for Sam was obviously business. Sam had a reputation for being miserable and a loner, yet the few times we did cross paths Sam always greeted me warmly, and we talked on length over a few drinks. However we rarely brought up the subject of our early days. On my part I did not want to remind, or embarrass Sam of his impoverished childhood. Perhaps Sam also felt the same way, but the one thing that has always amazed me, considering the terrible conditions that they had all endured, was the fact that Sam, alongside his brothers and sisters, all prospered in later life.

CHAPTER 9

HI HO, HI HO, IT'S OFF TO WORK I GO

By the time we had reached the age of thirteen we were all officially allowed to have part time employment. We saw very little of Eric now, because Eric in his spare time, besides studying, was working at his parents' butchers shop. Dave has I have explained we never bothered with. Surprisingly, and against his mum's wishes, Pete had acquired a job on Saturdays and in the school holidays, for a local fishmonger on a mobile shop that toured the villages around the Scarborough area. Pete enjoyed the work, although he took umbrage to my nickname for him 'Cod head Harrison' Sam, although commandeered by his dad to help supplement his boozing money, still found the time to work diligently at an array of jobs for himself, although keeping any money he had earned well away from his dad. I myself had found employment with a morning and evening newspaper round, but after about six months I acquired a new and better paid job as a part time errand boy for a family run grocery business.

'Albert Watson and Son' were a local grocer's shop that had begun trading before the first world war, and after Albert's death the business was carried on by Tom, his son, who at nearly seventy years of age still ran the business with his own son Dennis, who was married with two children and lived in a flat above the premises. Barry, a school friend, served behind the counter on a Saturday and in the school holidays, and it was Barry who had alerted me about the vacancy for an errand boy.

The internal of the shop was quite large and the shelves and cupboards were stocked with every kind of grocery item. The shop counter ran for nearly the full length of the shop. Three steps up from the shop floor; a door led into a small cubicle with a glass frontage that overlooked the shop

floor, and this was the sole domain of old Tom Watson. Tom wore thick black framed spectacle and with his grey thinning hair matched by a grey bushy moustache, to me he resembled an old bespectacled walrus. Tom was short and stout and he always wore a white overall, and if not serving behind the counter he would be sitting in his cubicle scrutinising any paper work, or glaring miserably through the cubicle window. As the name suggests my actual job was to deliver boxes of groceries to local customers on an old delivery bicycle which had a large deep basket at the front of the bike where the cardboard boxes of groceries were carried, however if no orders were waiting for me Tom could not bear to see me standing about and would give me any menial job to justify my wage. His son Dennis Watson, was different in most ways to his grumpy, miserable, old father. Dennis was a tall slim, well mannered, and a pleasant man. Behind the counter a door led to a small store room, whose shelves were packed with packets of spices, salt, flour, rice, and numerous other grocery items. Whenever Tom thought that I had nothing to do he would order me to the store room, to make up packets of sugar, or dried fruit The sugar was stored in a large paper sack, and with a large scoop I would pour the sugar into a one or two pound dark blue paper bag, weigh the bag on a pair of brass scales, fold the top over, and then stack the packets on a shelve. The dried fruits, raisins, sultanas, and mixed peels were stored separately in flat cardboard boxes, and the same weighing procedure as the sugar would be repeated but with a smaller scoop, of course I always sampled the fruit first. In the store room a trap door led down to a lowly cellar where all the empty spare cardboard boxes would be thrown into, and again if not busy I would be ordered down to the cellar to unfold the boxes and tie them into bundles, and to generally tidy up. I had now joined the local junior library, and enjoyed reading, so sometimes I took my latest book with me to work, and when working in the cellar, after attacking the cardboard boxes with gusto I would settle down to read my book, and every now and then I would rustle a cardboard box with my feet to make a noise in case of movement of the 'walrus,' creeping above in the store room. Barry and I shared the same type of humour, and even Dennis at times would joke and laugh along with us, but not Tom. One day after Tom after had given me my list of deliveries, he began to walk back to his cubicle, I crept up close behind him, with my tongue out and pulling faces. Barry was sniggering, when Tom suddenly stopped, turned around abruptly, and I collided into him. Tom shaking his head, glared at me and muttered.

"Daft as a brush, daft as a b----- brush."

Another time I entered the shop after making some deliveries, the shop was empty except for Barry who was stood by himself at the counter. Quickly scanning the shop and seeing that the cubicle was empty, I whispered to Barry.

"Where's the walrus gone, looking for some fish"?

Barry didn't reply, he simply gave a large grin and looked downwards, however my own smile quickly disappeared as Tom`s face slowly appeared from beneath the counter, accompanied by a tutting noise, and as Tom rose up he snarled.

"No, the walrus has not gone looking for fish, now get out and get those other orders delivered sharpish, or you`ll get the toe of my boot up your backside."

Whenever there were some heavy, or a lot of orders to deliver 'Bessie' was brought out of semi-retirement. Bessie was a very old dilapidated van that should have been surrendered to the scrap yard many years previous, however Tom, always thinking of money, even though he moaned at any money spent on repairs to Bessie, refused to replace the van. Archie Crabshaw a local odd job man was hired to deliver any large and heavy orders in Bessie, and it was Archie who had named the van Bessie. Archie was married with six children, he was small and thin, and always seemed to be wearing the same old, dark green patched up jersey under a brown dirt stained overall, and wearing black boots with the left boot's tongue missing, and sporting an old flat hat that he firmly squashed over his head. I was always pleased to see Archie as he brightened up my day. Archie always had the obliging cigarette dangling in his nicotine stained mouth. Whenever Archie was brought in I was ordered to accompany him, although I only rode in the back of the van only once. What with the clanking, the shaking, and the overbearing smell of petrol fumes it was an experience that I did not want to repeat. So after that first ride I would always ride in the front with Archie, although I had to hold tightly onto the door handle with one hand while kneeling on the floor, because there was no passenger seat. Driving at its maximum speed of 25m.p.h. while coughing and bellowing out black smoke, Archie, wrestling with Bessie's very stiff steering wheel and double clutch, and with a cigarette permanently dangling on the edge of his lips, would curse angrily above Bessie's droning engine.

"B------ old rust bucket, it's like driving a f-------- sardine can. I keep telling the tight old b----- to get a new van but will he listen, oh no will he b------ hell"

Then casting a glance at me, and a grin appearing on his face Archie added.

"Do ya know young un, old Tom is so tight he is the only bloke I know who can peel an orange in his trouser pocket so he doesn't have to offer a piece to anyone."

Tossing his head back he laughed loudly at his own joke. Then coughing and spluttering Archie, his face distorted as he crunched the gear stick into the top gear, spit the fag end out through the drivers door's open window, and replaced it with another cigarette. I had many laughs with Archie on the deliveries, and also with Barrie and Dennis at the shop, and disregarding his sour attitude, old Tom could provoke humour simply by his actions and the things he would say. I worked at 'Albert Watson and Son' for the final year before I left school, and although it was only a short period in my life I still hold fond memories, and spare a smile at the time I was employed by 'The Walrus'.

In the early sixties unless you were going onto higher education the official school leaving age was fifteen years of age, and depending on the date of your birthday you could leave school either at Summer, Christmas, or Easter terms. I was due to leave school at Christmas, however a few months before that final Christmas; dad had asked me what type of work I intended to do after leaving school. Well the truth was that like most of my friends I had never really considered my future. At the time there were an abundance of jobs and in some cases needing very few qualifications. However dad was adamant that whatever occupation I chose would be fine by him, but one thing he was certain about was the fact that I would have to have a trade, and no dead end job. For a few days I pondered on what to do, and the fact that Ted was a bricklayer and liked being in the building trade made up my mind. Dad had been a well-known hard-working builder's labourer both before and after the war, and although he had sold his window cleaning round and he was now the caretaker of St Peters Roman Catholic school he still had many friends in the building trade. Arthur Payne, a close friend of dad was now a General foreman at one of the largest building contractors in Scarborough. Arthur had arranged an interview with the management for me. After the interview with Joe Black the general manager, in which I had provided my end of term report and a surprise glowing reference from the headmaster Mr Davis (Dizzy), I was accepted as a bricklayer's apprentice.

On a very cold Monday morning in early January 1962, I began my first day's work as a bricklayer's apprentice. Little did I know at the time that I was to spend the next forty seven years in the building trade. A new pub was being built on North Marine Road opposite the Scarborough Cricket Club. The pub was to be called 'The Cricketers', and that was my first day's initiation into the building trade. The new construction was at the time only at ground level, the General foreman was dad's old friend Arthur Payne, and the foreman bricklayer with whom Arthur had entrusted me with was Harry Fenwick, a tall portly man with a small moustache, who always wore a black beret. Joe Black the general manager of the firm was a bricklayer by trade who had worked his way up to his present position. Joe was a tough talking forthright clever business man who held no favourites among his workforce. The firm was well known for its abundant of apprentices, although it was not because of Joe's kindness, but for his desire for profit. Joe would entrust the apprentice with a trusted foreman tradesman for about a month, in either bricklaying, joinery, plumbing or electrics. At the end of that period Joe would seek the foreman's appraisal of his charge, if the foreman's opinion were negative the apprentice would without doubt be dismissed the following week. However if the foreman's judgement was favourable the apprentice would be issued with a kit of tools, for which a few shillings a week would be deducted from his weekly pay until the bill was settled. On Joe's insistence the apprentice would be initiated into his chosen trade straight away and not with any mundane work such as cleaning up, or running errands for any of the workforce. This was not a soften of Joe's heart, but an apprenticeship lasted for six years, from the age of fifteen until twenty one, so by the time the apprentice had reached eighteen years of age he would be doing a man's work, yet only receiving half the wage of a fully qualified tradesman. However for the apprentice it meant a continual chance to learn, and shape his skills while his apprenticeship continued. The site for 'The Cricketers' faced the Scarborough cricket ground, but the rear of the site was approximately thirty metres above sea level and the North Marine Drive, which ran between the South and North bays. Although I was clothed thickly for the winter months ahead, nothing had prepared me for the snow, and icily north easterly winds that cut through me to the bone. That first day I was instructed by Harry or big Harry as he was known on the firm, to watch and learn as he constructed a brick wall. I stared in fascination at how Harry picked up the mortar with his trowel from the wooden mortar board, and then with a simple twist of his wrist he spread the mortar evenly over the course of bricks, and then he laid the following course of bricks. After about an hour of watching Harry pick up, spread the mortar, and lay the bricks, Harry instructed a labourer to put some mortar on a wooden board, and then I was ordered to practice with an old brick trowel belonging to Harry; the technique of rolling the mortar, picking it up, and spreading it evenly on the edge of the wooden mortar board. After nearly an hour of continual practice I considered myself to be quite efficient in the technique of picking up and spreading of the mortar, so in a hail of snow and biting wind, my hands and feet numb with cold, I announced to Harry,

"I have learnt how to spread the mortar; now Harry."

Harry, his moustache twitching, bellowed.

"LEARNT IT, LEARNT IT, I've been in the game for nearly f------- forty years and I'm still learning. Now you just keep on practicing you young b-------- until I tell you to stop."

Believe me when I tell you that I spent the rest of that freezing day, hour after boring hour, on that same wooden board, practicing how to spread the mortar.

One thing that I did learn quickly about the building trade was the quick and dry humour that excised on the building sites, and also the cross section of men that graced the trade, from the intelligent and educated, to the downright idiotic and slightly insane. Of the many tales and stories I have told, or I have heard over the years, people have sworn that I have made them up, or at the very least exaggerated the situations, but please believe me when I tell you that everything I write; apart from changing the people's names, is one hundred percent true. I am not going to explain the intricate, or go in to the details of my apprenticeship, but only to state that I served my time mostly with tradesmen of the finest quality in the old way of bricklaying, while at the same time learning about new techniques and materials that were then emerging. In those days of serving an apprenticeship in bricklaying, you also learned not only how to build in the correct and proper manner, but also in reading building plans, and how to use setting out levels. We also attended the Technical College one day a week to further our building education.

For two years of my apprenticeship I worked with Victor a skilled bricklayer, who was also skilled in stonework. Learning, and assisting with Victor, I helped build a number of brick, and stone buildings. Through Victor I learned the art of building in stone, which brought me many rewards in my later life, both financial, and in personal satisfaction. Though apprentices argued, and sometimes we fought among themselves, and clowned about a lot, all the apprentices were generally respectful to the older generation, mind you if we were not a smack around the ear soon made you see sense, regardless of how tough you or your mates thought you were. Although there was a lot of hard work involved, in some dreadful weather conditions, there was always something to make me smile. I have selected only a small percentage of the many comical situations and sometimes strange characters that were around at that present time.

Harry Fenwick, or big Harry as he was known by the rest of the workforce, was a very neat skilful bricklayer foreman, but he was also very self-conscious and insecure. Harry always seemed to think that people were talking about him behind his back. That first week Harry opened a paper bag and he gave me a toffee and then looking fervently around in case anybody might be listening he whispered,

"Son, if you hear anybody talking about me; or criticising of any of my work, just you come over to me and let me know, and I will give you another toffee."

Of course at the first opportunity I went straight to four bricklayers that were working nearby and repeated what Harry had mentioned. A small and wiry bricklayer called Sam sent me back to Harry with this message.

"Sam said that he was standing at the bar in the 'Lions Head' at the weekend, and somebody was slagging you off something awful. The bloke said; 'That Harry Fenwick couldn't lay a table, never mind b------ bricks."

After retelling Sam's tale, Harry's eyes widened, and in a fury he stormed over to Sam and roared,

"Sam! Who the b------ hell was slagging me off, because I will go to the 'Lions Head' this weekend and break his f----- neck and--____.

Suddenly Harry stopped yelling, and looking confused he added,

"Anyway Sam, where is the 'Lions Head'?"

Sam working diligently away, and with not a hint of a smile on his face, turned round to face Harry and replied,

"Well Harry, I would guess it's about six feet from its arse."

Another day, with a chilling wind blowing, I was assisting Harry and another bricklayer in building a brick wall, when the architect of the project came on to the site, he stopped directly besides Harry. The architect smiled at Harry, and then deep in thought he began to gaze around the site. Harry looked at the architect a number of times, and then with a frown on his face, he growled.

"Well! What the hell is wrong with my work? Come on I want to know?"

The architect was completely confused, and he politely replied,

"Err --I'm sorry what did you say?"

However, Harry had by now completely convinced himself that the innocent architect was critical of Harry's work, so he continued with his verbal onslaught.

"Nobody has complained before of my work, and I have been in the building trade for nearly forty years and if you think you can do any b------ . better here's my trowel, and---"

Giggling, the other bricklayer and myself retreated behind the wall and laughed loudly, while Harry continued his verbal onslaught on the poor baffled architect.

After Easter, a friend and former class mate, joined me at the firm, as a bricklayer apprentice. In fact from Friarage School a number pupils came to work within the building industry, so it seems that Friarage School was a conveyor belt for the Scarborough building industry. The first building site where my friend and I worked together was on the construction of a new Police station, and Police houses in Pickering, a small country town approximately twenty miles from Scarborough. A few local workers were recruited from Pickering itself, but the majority of the workforce came from Scarborough. A large transit van was provided, with planks in the back of the van for seats, and also a large lorry with a temporary wooden hut on the back of the lorry, fastened down by ropes, which was used to transport the Scarborough workers to and from Pickering. Most of the men boarded the van and lorry at the firm's depot, but a few of the men; like Harry were picked up en-route. The lorry driver could not see anybody boarding, or unboarding, the lorry because of the wooden hut, so the signal for the driver to stop or to go, was to stamp a foot on the lorry's back floor. One evening Harry, when he had reached his home destination stamped his foot on the lorries floor and as the lorry stopped, Larry cocked one of his wide legs over the tail board, and with a bag containing his flask and lunch box slung over his shoulder, he carefully began to descend down the short ladder that was fastened on to the lorry's tail board. But because of his huge bulk Harry was having difficulty reaching the ground. A joiner winked across at my mate and myself and stamped his foot hard on the lorry's floor. The lorry slowly started to move forward while Harry, clinging onto the small ladder, with one leg on the road and the other leg stuck on the ladder, began to frantically hop and down on the road as the lorry started to pick up speed. Most of the occupants, myself included, started laughing at the sight of poor Harry's face which could be seen just peering over the tail board, contorted in fear and helplessness, but another more concerned man stamped hard on the floor and the lorry stopped abruptly to a halt. Harry with a yell fell onto the road like Humpty Dumpty. The next day Harry furiously scoured around the site trying to find the person who had caused his ordeal and embarrassment, although, strangely, nobody had a clue, or even knew who the culprit was.

Alex Duckworth was a bricklayer who originated from Sheffield. Alex was in his mid-fifties,

he was of small build, and he wore thick horn-rimmed glasses. There was a debate among the men on the firm if Alex was sane or just slightly unbalanced, but there was no doubting that he was one of the strangest characters on the firm. Many a time Alex would sit cross legged, crouched under the wooden dining table at tea break, or lunch time, making loud animal noises However, the men at ease with his actions, just carried on regardless with their breaks. Alex also had an annoying habit of repeating certain sayings time and time again, that in itself was bad enough, but usually what he said was complete utter nonsense, an example being.

"How many sticks of rhubarb in a rice pudding? If you went far, how far would you come back again? "Do two lefts make a right?"

These are just a few of the ridiculous sayings that Alex would spout during the course of the day. Those sayings at first seemed funny, but after hearing them day after day they became repetitively boring. Sand and cement, plus a measure of lime, was the mortar mix generally used at the time for bonding the bricks together The bricklayers used a variety of names to describe the mix such as mortar, gear, muck, and darbo. Alex, much to the other workers annoyance would sing out continuously while he was working

"Bricks and lime all the time, bricks and lime all the time"

One day Eric, a young muscular labourer snarled at Alex.

"I'm b----- sick of hearing you say 'bricks and lime all the time' if you say it once more I'm going to throw you off this b----- scaffold."

Alex didn't reply, but simply gave Eric an idiotic grin, however he did stop singing the verse. Later in the day Eric was working on the ground level about four metres below where we were working, when Alex leaned over the scaffold and shouted out Eric's name, and then he cupped his hands around his mouth and pretended to shout, but no words came out of Alex`s mouth. Eric put his hand to his ears and shouted back up

"What did you say Alex?"

Alex repeated this action several times but each time Eric was getting more and more aggravated, so he cupped his hands around his mouth and shouted back up

"Speak up I can't b-------- hear you."

Alex just smiled and once more he repeated his silent action. Exasperated, Eric bounded up two ladders to reach the scaffold where we were working, and walking up to him Eric snarled breathlessly at Alex.

"What the hell did you say Alex, I can't hear you from down there?"

Alex gave a grin, cupped his hands once more around his mouth, and bellowed loudly.

I SAID BRICKS AND LIME ALL THE F--------- TIME."

Eric instead of being angry, simply smiled, shook his head, and burst into laughter

Alex was a good worker, but his work at times were appalling. One day the manager Joe Black came onto the site, and seeing the cement smeared wall that Alex had just built he growled.

"What a b----- load of rubbish, without doubt this is the most disgraceful piece of work I have seen in a long time, Alex, you're finished, come to the office for your cards at the end of the week."

Unperturbed Alex just smirked, and replied.

"Well I can show you a wall that is far worse than this one Joe, and it's on this job as well."

Joe growled back.

"Well I can't believe there is any work worse than this rubbish, but if you show me the wall, and tell me who built it, then I might let you keep your job."

Alex took Joe to the other side of the site, and pointed to a brick wall that was not only crooked and stained, but out of level as well. Joe stared at the brick wall with disgust, then turning to Alex, he growled.

"Well, I don't believe it, but you're b------ right, it's a disgrace, so tell me who was it that built this load of rubbish?"

Alex grinned, and pointing at his chest with pride, he replied.

"Me, do I still get to keep my job then Joe?"

In the building industry there are a lot of men who just seem to drift into the trade and then vanish just as quickly. There were many men, and incidents that I could recall, that would not only fill this chapter; but the rest of the book. However, there is one particular labourer who comes to mind. I would be about eighteen at the time, and I had been entrusted to build a small extension with a labourer who had just started on the firm to assist me. The labourer was mixing the mortar in the cement mixer to my instructions when Arthur Payne walked onto the job. Arthur and I began discussing details about the job, when the labourer approached us, and just stood looking over our shoulders with an idiotic smile on his face

Arthur looked annoyingly a couple of times at the labourer, before he growled angrily.

"Don't just b----- stand there looking like an idiot, put some muck on this mortar board"

The labourer looked puzzlingly at Arthur.

"You what?"

Arthur shook his head and growled.

"Are you b------ deaf man? I said put some muck on that mortar board."

Arthur and I walked around the small extension talking. About five minutes later we returned, and we both stared unbelievingly at the piled-up mortar board.

The labourer had literary taken Arthur to his word, because piled up on the mortar board was soil, grass sods, small pieces of broken brick, splinters of wood, and placed at the pinnacle of it all was an empty cigarette packet.

Arthur scowled, while I burst into laughter, but the labourer simply shrugged his shoulders and
said.

"Well you did say fill up the mortar board with muck, didn't you?"

Arthur with his hands on his hips, stood glaring at the labourer, who unperturbed.

was slowly walking back towards the cement mixer. Arthur looked back at me and growled,

"I just don't know if he is completely thick, or if he is taking the p---"

Bill was a small wiry looking labourer, who always wore an old black army beret, married with eight children, Bill or 'Mad Bill as he was called, certainly lived up to his name. One lunch time Bill complained (with many swear words) that he was annoyed with the stray cat that two of his daughters had adopted because, as he put it.

"The f------ thing keeps getting under the sofa and p----ing."

Bill continued his verbal onslaught of the cat for the next couple of days. However after no comments for about a week, one lunch break, Roy, an electrician, asked Bill.

"Hey Bill, you haven't said anything lately about your cat, are you still having trouble with it?"

Bill looked up and grinned.

"No Roy, not now, because the cat won't be going under the b------- sofa no more that's for sure?

"Why? Have you got rid of the cat.?" Asked Roy

Bill's smile grew wider, and he tapped the side of his nose with the side of his finger and said wisely.

"No, I sawed the legs off the f----- sofa."

From the late sixties onward there was a tremendous surge of work in the building trade both in and around the Scarborough area, constructing new buildings, extensions to factories, and also national building companies were building dozens of new houses and bungalows in a number of the new estates, as well as the villages around the Scarborough area, but more importantly firms were offering big wages and bonuses. The firm in which I worked did not bind their apprentices at the time, so a number of apprentices had decided to leave the company to reap the financial rewards. I had decided, much to my dad's protest, to leave also, but not for the money. My present company dealt mainly with big contracts, but I wanted to learn other skills in the trade so after a very heated debate with Joe Black I handed in my notice, and found further employment with a much smaller local building firm which had been established for over fifty years. The firm was a family run firm that specialised in small building, and joinery works, but also doubled up as funeral directors. At the time the majority of the men at the firm were mostly in their late fifties and sixties, and the majority of them had worked at the firm since leaving school, all were exceptional good tradesmen, but most of the workforce were submissive and terrified of losing their jobs, which I suppose to them, to have a permanent wage and continual employment was still regarded as a privilege. The present owner of the firm was a grey haired, charming gentleman, who knew very little concerning the building trade, so he relied on his faithful foremen's and workforce to carry him through. However he was a top class funeral director and also a member of a local church. I was then nineteen years of age and I belonged to an entirely different generation, upbeat, confident, and like most of my friends I took my work seriously, but not the world in general. So apart from our age difference, to myself most of the workforce seem to come from an alien world regarding almost everything. The present owner's father before the Second World War; was owed a debt by a farmer, the farmer did repay that debt, but with a section of land situated about three miles out of Scarborough. Although his father had died some years previous, the present owner was not only a successful funeral director but also he had a keen eye to financial matters. Seeing the tremendous surge in the building of new homes, he decided to develop and build some new bungalows on the land that he had acquired. However, with only a minimal work force for all this extra work, he had no option but to employ more men, hence not only my own employment, but about a dozen other new workers were also employed.

At first it was a bit daunting having to learn plastering, tiling, roof work, etc. (jobbing work as it was known) and although it was different I enjoyed the work. One day in my first month at the firm, a new labourer and I were working near the firm's building yard and office, and so as it was nearly lunch time we decided to have our half hour lunch break in the joiner's workshop. When we stepped inside the ground floor of the joiners shop we were greeted by stacks of different lengths, and thickness`s of wood, boxes of screws, nails, and an assortment of tins, boxes, and bags of building materials. Above in the work shop we heard the sound of banging and scrapping, yet strangely no sound of any voices. On reaching the top of the stairs the sight that greeted us could have come straight from the previous century. The workshop was very badly lit and foreboding, and working diligently but silently, besides the thick old wooden work benches, surrounded by shavings, screws, and small pots of glue, were five joiners. Standing at the end of one of the benches was Charlie, the joiner foreman, who had been working for the firm since leaving school (probably about two hundred years to my reckoning) Charlie was in his sixties, small, grizzled, and with a face that looked as though he had been sucking lemons all morning On the wall behind Charlie, ticking monotonously was an old large pendulum clock. Nobody raised their heads, or even exchanged our pleasant greetings, in fact it was as though we were invisible. Pointing at the clock, the new labourer called out cheerfully.

"Come on lads it's lunch time."

However, no one made a reply, but with heads still bent down they carried on working. A few seconds later Charlie glared menacingly at the labourer and myself, and then, instead of looking up at the big pendulum clock behind him, he pompously took out a fob watch from his overall pocket, stared at it, and simply snarled

"Dinner"

Without another word Charlie walked across the room and down the stairs. Only then did the

other joiners reach for their lunch bags and sit down at the benches. To say the conversations was dull, was an overstatement. Though I was young, and I knew only too well that our interests were vastly different, I was unprepared for the talk of coffins, funerals, worrying about the jobs, and all the work that had to be done, with also plenty of back biting, and bitching about the other workers on the firm. Needless to say that was the first, and last time, apart from necessity, that I visited the joiner's workshop again. I will not dwell in depth on the work that I was involved with as this could become boring. However, as previously mentioned I was to come in contact during my years in the building trade with many interesting characters, and some of these characters and comic situations I recall now are only a few of what occurred during my period at this firm.

The majority of the workers were of a dull and boring nature, however a couple of the workmen on the firm did possess a sense of humour, one particular joiner Jack, had been employed with the firm for about eight years, even so he was still considered a recent recruit by the older workforce. Jack also doubled up as a pall bearer for any funerals that the firm conducted. One story even now; although in some ways it is perhaps sad and disrespectful, but it still makes me smile. I shall try to re-tell the story as Jack had told me it all those years ago.

"I had been working on the funeral side of the firm for a couple of years, but I was still regarded as a novice, when old Bill Horncastle who had been with the firm well before the war, and who actually died two years ago, came up to me on an extension of a house that we were doing and said that he wanted me to go with him to pick up a body of an old man who had just died the night before. Anyway we went in an old hearse to a little small squat cottage to pick up the body. We knocked on the door and the old man's wife answered, and after a polite conversation in which she said that her husband had died in bed that previous night and the doctor had said that it was a heart attack. So we took the shell (an old wooden coffin that was used to transport the body back to the chapel of rest) up to the bedroom of the cottage. Then we put the old man's body inside the shell, but when we tried to take the shell back down the stairs we couldn't manage it with the body in it as well, because the staircase was too narrow and winding, so we returned back to the bedroom. Taking off his flat cap and scratching his head for a while, Bill told me to help him lift the old man back out of the shell, and to lay him on the bedroom floor. Then Bill bent down and fastened some thick cloth around the man's head. Standing up he told me to go down the stairs to the front room, close the door and talk to the old woman, but no matter what I heard, on no account was I to let the old woman come out of the front room. Anyway there I was talking to the old woman, when suddenly there was a dull thud, and then another thud, the old widow just looked at me; and asked me what my friend was doing. Well, I had guessed straight away that Bill was dragging the old man's body slowly down the stairs one step at a time. Anyway I just didn`t know what the hell to say so I just sort of muttered to the old woman that my mate was bringing down the coffin, but she wanted to know why I wasn`t giving my friend a hand, so again I sort of muttered a flimsy sort of excuse. But I think she knew something was not right, because you should have seen the b------- look the old woman gave me. The bumping suddenly stopped. The old woman was now angry and pushed past me and opened the door into the hallway. I was in a right b---- state in case what she might see, but by then thank God, Bill had managed to get the old man down the stairs and into the shell and closed the lid, all by himself. Later, when we were driving back to the Chapel of Rest I turned to Bill and said

"Well Bill, if the poor old bugger isn't dead by now; he'll have one hell of an f------- headache when he wakes up."

On the building site there were to be a number of semidetached bungalows constructed, and although they were selling as fast as the firm could build them, the boss would only build one pair of bungalows at a time, and only then when other work was scarce. As I have already stated the tradesmen were of the highest calibre, and this showed in the work that was being produced.

As for myself I was getting the best of both worlds, general brickwork, plastering, tiling, roof work, and installing fireplaces. But with the amount of work increasing the firm had also set on a number of apprentices.

Paul was a plump lad who had just been employed as a bricklayer's apprentice, although a pleasant lad he was extremely dense. Ron the bricklayer foreman, who had been working for the firm for over forty years; had taken an instant dislike to Paul, perhaps that was because of the way he had behaved the previous week. There had been an horrific storm the week before and there was a vast amount of roofing repairs that had to be done, so most of the tradesmen and labourers had been brought off the other jobs and channelled into the roof repairs, except for Ron, myself, Raymond a labourer, and Paul, who had just started his first day on the site. Paul just stood looking at Ron and myself all the morning while we were constructing the brick foundations. Ron had given Paul a number of small jobs to do, however Paul seemed to be in a world of his own, and after a short time he would return and once again just stand there watching Ron and myself. It was about fifteen minutes to our lunch break and Ron, who was now getting more agitated with Paul by the minute, ordered him to go to the cabin and to put on the kettle for our tea. After about ten minutes Paul had not returned, so Ron told Raymond to find out what Paul was doing. Raymond quickly returned doubled over with laughter, Ron angrily asked Ray of Paul`s whereabouts, the labourer holding his side and laughing replied.

"He's still in the cabin, and you won't believe this Ron, but he`s just gone through a full box of matches trying to light the Kettle."

Again, Raymond had another bout of laughter. For a few seconds Ron looked at Raymond, and digested his answer, then he suddenly rasped

Light the kettle Light the kettle! But it's a b-------
electric kettle."

Raymond in between bouts of more laughter spluttered.
"Exactly."

After our dinner break Raymond went to the cement mixer to mix some more mortar, while Ron and myself, with Paul dawdling behind us, returned to the brick foundations. The mortar on the boards had dried, so Ron ordered Paul to fetch some water to make it more durable, however Paul looked baffled and he asked.

"What in?"

Ron's face contorted in anger, as he spluttered

"In a f-------- empty cement bag you stupid b----- idiot, what the hell do you think in?"

Paul looking perplexed, just walked away, while Ron, with his back to me grumbled.to himself.

"The thick idiot, there is about half a dozen buckets on the site and he asks, what in?"

A few minutes later I looked up in amazement as Paul, staggered slowly down the site clutching a bulging paper cement bag, with water seeping through its cover. Paul stopped besides Ron, who was bent over in a trench with his back to Paul, and with his two hands gripped tightly around the neck of the cement bag Paul passed it over to Ron saying.

"Here's your water Ron."

Ron turned around with his arms outstretched, but his eyes widened in surprise, as in complete surprise he took the bulging bag from Paul's hands. At that precise moment the bag burst open drenching a shocked Ron. I leaned against trench side and burst into laughter while Ron, absolutely livid, screamed abuse, not only at a confused Paul but also at me for laughing at Ron's predicament.

The firm was booming with work, and like myself new workers had been employed. Another bricklayer Danny, was only a few years older than myself, and he shared my interests and my humour, plus, he was also a good; and hardworking tradesman. The owner of the firm was in his mid-fifties, and with his silver hair and tall slim features, coupled with his smooth funeral director's manner he was the pin up boy for all the old maidens at the church of which he attended. One of his admirers from his congregation was Mrs. Cassidy, a pleasant timed widow, but also a very shrewd business woman, and had acquired an old worn down, but large property, which she intended to refurbish and turn into flats, she had entrusted the firm to do the renovation work. Although Mrs. Cassidy had a shrewd business brain, she was also very kind and friendly, and she would visit the Property every day. Because of the amount of work on the firm the workmen were constantly being moved around from one job to another, so it happened that one day at Mrs. Cassidy's property, there was only Danny and myself, a labourer called Phil, and Frank, a joiner who had been employed by the firm for over thirty five years. Frank was tall slim, with a hooked nose and very beady eyes. Frank was very integrated into the firm, one might say that he was overwhelmed, and turned into a quivering wreck by any appearance of the boss. One day Danny and I, with the labourer assisting, were bricking above a new steel girder we had fitted over a down stairs room, while Frank was busily patching up the old staircase, when just after lunch Mrs. Cassidy appeared. Whenever Mrs. Cassidy visited the property she would call out softly.

"It's only me"

But Frank, would instantly stop anything he was doing, and acting as a none appointed foreman he would take it upon himself to assist Mrs. Cassidy around the property, and to personally conduct and grovel to her, while explaining every little detail of the progress, probably hoping to integrate himself into her and the bosses good books. All that morning his tools lay scattered on the stairs, where he had been busily engaged in his repairs. Meanwhile Danny and I, about every half hour would take it in turns to shout up the staircase in a soft squeaky voice.

"It's only me."

At first Frank answered in a very polite and condescending voice

"Alright Mrs. Cassidy. Now you just stay where you are, while I gather up my tools, and make sure everything is safely out of your way before you come up the stairs, we don't want any accidents do we?"

From down below, sniggering, we could hear Frank quickly running up and down the landings and stairs, gathering his tools. However after a couple of times Frank had grown wise to our scam, and he would angrily shout down abuse to Danny and myself. Later that afternoon Mrs. Cassidy did come to visit the house, and approached Danny and myself, as we were still busy working on the new steel girder After a few minutes of polite conversation, she walked to the bottom of the stairs, and on hearing Frank's banging, she called out softly.

"It's only me"

From two floors above Frank growled.

"What do you want, a f------ medal you old bat? Anyway why don't you ask the boss about any spare coffins that's going cheap."

Frank laughed at his own joke, before he added.

"You two lads won't b------ fool me anymore, I`lll make damn sure of that"

Frank, thinking that it was Danny and I who were still fooling about, now began ridiculing Mrs. Cassidy even more. Danny and I grinned at each other. However, Mrs. Cassidy seemingly unperturbed, began to slowly climb the stairs, Danny and myself, keeping well out sight, slowly followed her, while Frank, still laughing, carried on with his abuse. As Mrs. Cassidy rounded the next landing she came into full view with Frank. To his absolute horror Frank realised it was indeed Mrs. Cassidy. Frank stared in shock and disbelief, while swallowing a number of times, the colour literally draining from his face. Danny and I crept silently back downstairs before looking at each other; and breaking into hysterical laughter. A few minutes later we could hear Frank, grovelling even more than usual to Mrs.

Cassidy, while walking about between the upstairs rooms. Some minutes later Mrs. Cassidy after descending the stairs, put her head in the doorway and bade a cheerfully goodbye to Danny, Phil the labourer, and myself, before she walked away and closed the front door behind her. After a few seconds of silence, from upstairs, we heard a groan, and then a loud yell followed by the sound of feet pounding down the staircase. Suddenly framed in the doorway, there stood Frank, a thick piece of timber in his hand, his face red, and his beady eyes bulging. Frank lunged at Danny and myself, however before he could catch us, Danny and I quickly ran out of the back door, through the back garden, and leapt over the low boundary wall. Ten minutes later, we crept back to the house, and looked through the open kitchen window. Frank was standing, still with the piece of wood still in his hand, angrily talking to the labourer. Danny tapped gently on the window pane, and as Frank turned towards the window Danny smiled, and said in a soft squeaky voice

"Yoo-hoo. It's only me."

When I look back at the two building firms of my apprenticeship, I know that I received a good grounding in the all-round skill of a bricklayer, from tradesmen of the highest calibre. Yet their fear of the sack, and of the treatment and the complete disregard of their workforces by their Employers, is something I have never forgotten. When I was twenty-one years of age I met and then got engaged to Irena, my future wife, and I decided that; to support a wife, and hopefully a family, I needed a good income. Now that I was a fully skilled tradesman, I reasoned that if I was honest, and worked hard to the best of my abilities, I also should receive just payment, and so began my journey through the building trade.

156

CHAPTER 10

THE SIXTIES: MUSIC, VENUES, AND FASHION

The music in the early sixties was bland to say the least. Rock and Roll which had revolutionized popular music in the mid to late fifties with recording stars such as Little Richard, Buddy Holly, the Everly brothers, and the biggest influence of them all Elvis Presley, had peaked. At the time, Francis my elder sister, had a big record collection of most of those artists, and I too, although still in my childhood liked the sound of that music. However by the time I had left school popular music had changed. Elvis seemed to be more interested in mushy ballads, and the so-called British rock stars like Cliff Richard, Adam Faith, and Billy Fury were only pale imitations of the former American rock and roll pioneers. Once I had left school and started work I was interested not only in music, but clothes, and girls as well. When I began full time employment my starting pay was three pounds ten shillings (£3-50p) a week, and each following birthday of my apprenticeship I was to receive a pay rise, however Dad from the start told me to me hand over one pound ten shillings to my mum for my board, the rest I could keep. At the time two pounds could go a long way if you were careful, but unfortunately, I, like the rest of my mates was not careful with money. Cigarettes, clothes, and enjoying ourselves took care of most of our wages. I was paid on the Friday, however by Sunday night all my money had been spent. If you were under eighteen years of age, the pictures, (movies) coffee bars, or perhaps the Y.M.C.A, a club for boys, were the only places to go for most teenagers. Unfortunately if my money had expired until the following pay day, or I had managed to borrow something from my dad, the rest of the evenings would have to be spent with my parents watching the television, but this was boring so with four of my mates we would take turns visiting each other's houses, playing cards (usually with small stakes). At the time there were no radio stations for music apart from the B.B.C, but unfortunately none of their music programs catered for teenagers, so to satisfy our taste for pop music we turned to Radio Luxemburg. To tune into Radio Luxemburg for a decent signal was a time-consuming effort, for the dial on the radio had to be turned ever so slightly until a relatively audible sound could be obtained, even then the sound still wavered. Every Sunday tea time from 4 until 5 o'clock we would listen to 'Pick of the Pops' which played the week's top twenty pop records from the music charts. One memorable Sunday night as we played cards, laughing joking, and fooling about, the D.J. introduced a record that was to turn me into a big music fan for the rest of my life. Here, I have tried to recall much of that introduction.

(Quote) "Now, for a record at number six in the charts, with a great beat, here are four young lads from Liverpool called 'The Beatles' who recently had a top twenty hit with their first record 'Love Me Do', But now after only just being released two weeks ago, and absolutely storming up the charts to a certain number one, is their follow up record called 'Please, Please Me'".

As the first driving thudding beat, with a wailing mouth organ, followed by the rasping words blasted through the crackling radio, we all sat up and stared at each other, memorised at this so very different sound, and we were hooked. That record changed the face of popular music for ever. The Beatles turned the music world completely upside down, not just with their singing and music, but unlike most of the artists before, they actually wrote their own songs, and they looked, dressed, talked, and fooled about just like any other youth you could find in any town or city in England. No more the clean-cut well-groomed English or American boys with a polite manner, but just four, although extremely talented ordinary young men. This may sound crass, but this was where the sixties for me really began. The Beatles were the vanguard of the Mersey sound, and what was very soon to be, the British sound. The Beatles smashed aside what had always been the American domination of popular music on both sides of the Atlantic. Soon groups and singers were emerging not just from Liverpool, but from every corner of Britain. The groups like the music were different and exciting and they varied in both music and style. In Scarborough, before this teenage revolution, the music reflected the rest of the country because the groups were mainly of the Cliff Richards and The Shadows type, which for me was boring, and unexciting. There were no discotheques, those were to come a few years later, so coffee bars were still the only the real meeting points for the younger generation. However there was one night for the Scarborough teenagers, the regular mid-week dance at the Olympia ballroom, opposite the beach on Foreshore Road. Hit records of the day were played, followed by the top group of the time in Scarborough, 'Jonty and The Strangers 'who were extremely good musicians and well liked, but they still performed the old type of popular music. However, in the following years new local younger groups with their own sets of fans began to emerge; to play this new music such as The Incas, The Moonshots, Electra, and many more. A New Year's Eve dance was always held at The Spa ballroom, featuring the old-fashioned Graham Pinkney Band, bow tied, and middle-aged musicians, playing dull middle of the road music. However, being a teenager and under eighteen years of age, but needing somewhere to celebrate the evening, the Spa at the time was the only venue to attended where both boys and girls could meet, also as an added attraction there was a bar, where, if you held your nerve and lied about your age, you could purchase alcohol. I was to be sixteen years old that January, and although I was unaware of it at the time, a new music revolution had just began, thank goodness it would be my last time at the Spa ballroom because many new venues would be opening in the years to come that would be catering for a new generations music and tastes

The emerging of all this music and new groups, had a profound affect all over the country, and Scarborough reflected this. New local groups were emerging all the time, and some church halls were even opening their doors and encouraging the music by having regular teenage dance nights. Now with money in my pocket I put more energy into my social life. As I was now working, I bought myself a record player on which I played L.Ps (albums) and 45s (single records) usually loud in my bedroom much to my parents disapproval. This was the start for my long love affair with music. Although not having any particular favourite group or singer, I amassed a large record collection with a wide taste in both artistes and sounds.

The upsurge of all these groups and singers in Britain, was a great boost for The Futurist picture house, which had lately converted to variety shows as well as showing movies. The Spa ballroom in Bridlington, about twenty miles from Scarborough was also becoming more popular, because record companies and promoters sent out tours to the theatres and ballrooms up and down the country, with a major recording group of the time topping the bill, adding two or three other chart hit artists, and perhaps a couple of unknown groups or singers to complete the bill, some of whom would later develop into top artists themselves. It was known as a 'Package Tour'. I saw many of the now legendary groups and singers appear on these tours, but unlike today's technology cover ups, most of the bands and singers recreated their sound on stage as on their records I was thrilled to see The Beatles at the beginning of their meteoric rise to world fame at The Futurist, but by seeing them I use the term lightly, because the screaming and noise from the audience was deafening, making their music none excitant, and my mates and I only caught glimpses of The 'Beatles' through the masses of swooning screaming females. I also deemed myself lucky to witness the sheer pulsating power of the rhythm and blues music with the five original 'Rolling Stones' also at the Futurist.

About three times a year The Bridlington Spa would hold an all-night dance on a Friday night, where a top recording group would head the bill, supplemented by about ten local groups. The doors would be opened at eight o'clock on the Friday evening and the music would continue nonstop until six thirty the following morning. Besides the music and dancing there was the added attraction of two large bars, and also a fried breakfast (if you could face it) could be purchased at six am, from the Spa's cafeteria the next morning. These Friday dances were very popular for the area's teenagers the doors being shut when it was deemed that the Spa was full. So gaining admission was a must, however there was a guaranteed way to gain admission. A week before the event we would purchase our tickets from Bernard Deans music shop in St Thomas street in Scarborough, which meant that, not only were you guaranteed admission, but after a half hour train journey from Scarborough you could spend some time in the

Bridlington pubs before venturing on to the Spa. My eighteenth birthday coincided with one of these dances in which 'The Kinks' were the headlined band. A few years later in the mid-sixties, Scarborough reflected the rest of the country, because teenagers had now become the centre of a cultural revolution in both music and fashion. British music now ruled the world, and even the once American dominated stage and film industries had succumbed to the great upsurge, with movies, musicals, and theatres, featuring young British actors and actresses who were later to become Icons in the world of show business.

The teenagers' hunger for pop music gave birth to pop programs on television which were created entirely for this new generation, such as Thank Your Lucky Stars, Ready Steady Go, and the pinnacle for fans and artists alike, 'Top Of The Pops'. Also, another revolution to evolve alongside this unsatisfied demand was the unlicensed pirate radio ships, which transmitted continuous pop music from off shore ships, one of which 217, operated near Scarborough in the North Sea. All this popular hysteria eventually forced the B.B.C. to create its own pop music station, produced entirely for younger listeners 'Radio One', which still survives to this day.

One of the first discothèques in England had opened in Scarborough, it was called 'The Scene'. And what a revolution, because until then dance halls were mostly the only places for music and dancing. The Scene was fantastic, the lighting were dim, but on the dance floor it was heaving with a fresh new generation dancing to continuous hit records of the day, and spinning, flashing lights, accompanying the pulsating new music The 'Scene' discothèque had been built on the site of the demolished old 'Bar Church' in Aberdeen Walk. However, only a few years later. Scene 2, situated above the Scene 1 was launched, feathering top groups of the day such as: Status Quo, The Searchers The Drifters, The Troggs, and many more. Also other Scarborough night clubs that were once the domain of an older cliental were now catering for teenagers. The 'Candle Light' was a night club situated at the bottom of Blands Cliff, close to the South bay beach, and it became a favourite haunt for many teenagers. 'The Candlelight' was on the inside exactly as the name suggests. There was a small dance floor that heaved under the strain of the dancing teenagers, and an even smaller stage on which a more in tune D.J. would play the latest hit records of the day, and sometimes a local pop group would perform. Around the sides of the club were chairs and tables, each table had a candle burning in an empty wine bottle, (health and safety laws were then not so stringent) obviously the bar and dance floor were always crowded. However, unless you arrived early a huge queue would be waiting to gain admission. A few years later the Candlelight transferred to larger premises near the town centre in Huntress Row. It was about this time, that apart from listening and dancing to the music, I also begun to pay more attention to the lyrics of songs, especially the graphic songwriters such as Lennon and McCartney, Bob Dylan, Paul Simon, Ray Davis, and Cat Stevens.

There was another night club that played continuous hit records, although having a much seedier interior, 'The 'Flamingo Club' situated in cellar, in an area of Scarborough called South Cliff. 'The Flamingo Club' was dark and dingy, with fishing nets and other oddments' hanging on the staircase and interior walls, which somehow added a sort of strange, mystic feel to the place. However on wet and rainy nights water would seep up through the stone paved floor, and in really heavy rainfalls even cascade down the concrete steps, yet, though less sophisticated than some of the other night clubs or discotheques, the Flamingo had an atmosphere all of its own and many great weekend nights were spent there. A bowling alley had been constructed above a block of new shops in Newborough; in the bottom end of the town, which also contained a new night club called the 'Le Chat Noir' (The Black Cat) which did not open until late evening, but lasted until the early hours of the next day, it had a resident blind piano player who played jazz music, chaperoned by his teenage daughter. Dimly lit and peaceful, it was a pleasant way to wind down at the end of a chaotic and exciting weekend. Further up the town, a few years later in Huntriss row near the new 'Candlelight' the 'Bier Keller' was opened. A flight of wooden stairs leading down from the street brought you to the basement, which like the name suggests was set out in a German style dance hall, complete with wooden benches and tables, with a large dance floor, and a bar that served English, or if you wanted German style beer, and it was always well attended. The clientele listened or danced to the latest music, either on tape, or performed by local groups. Like the Flamingo Club, the 'Bier Keller' had an atmosphere all of its own. In the summer months there were three pleasure boats operating from Scarborough harbour, taking passengers for a one hour cruise around the coastline, the Regal Lady, the Yorkshire Lady, and the largest, the Coronia. Every Friday night the Coronia set to sea for a two hour cruise filled with teenagers, belting out the latest pop music, plus a local pop group providing the live music. However after the first Friday night, and a very choppy cruise, my mates and I consumed little alcohol on any of the future dance trips. Every Christmas; an event is held in the bottom end of Scarborough on Boxing Day. The origins of the event began many years previous when a local trawler sank and all the crew perished. .A football game was organised by the fishing community and played on the south beach, with a collection being held with all the proceeds going to the deceased fishermen's dependents. Also in those days Christmas Day was a busy time for the women (just as it still is) but the following day, 'Boxing Day', was very different. Locally, it was known as 'Ladies Day'. All the women would dress up and meet in each other's homes, or in the sea front pubs. At first it was just the women, but times change and by the early sixties it was for not only the women but also included the men. New licensing laws had been introduced after the World War, and in Scarborough the public houses were strictly controlled, all the pubs were closed on both Christmas day, and on Boxing Day. However, the pubs down in the bottom end on Boxing Day were granted a special license from twelve noon until 2-30 pm on the afternoon (officially) although the rest of the town on Boxing Day was enveloped in a ghostly silence, but the bottom end was like a carnival day. Foreshore Road was heaving, but all the ice cream shops, crab stalls, fish restaurants, and amusement arcades were firmly closed for the winter months, except for 'The Harbour Bar' the ice cream parlour, which served not only ice cream, but with your coffee you could have a small measure of rum added; at no extra expense. Judging by the swarming crowds it could have been a hot August day not a cold snow swept December morning. A comic four-piece band, in a mish mash of gaudy clothes, and roughly applied makeup, played out of tune music. Following the comic band, other similar dressed men and women rattled tin buckets, in which the willing public tossed coins into, all the proceeds would go directly towards ''The Fishermen Wive's Fund' a local organisation that provided food hampers for the old folks living in the bottom end of town. On the sea-side of Foreshore Road, a line of pennies was placed along the kerb

165

edge, by the same willing public, the long line of pennies also going to the same charity. My friends and I would meet up at ten o'clock in the morning at one of our houses, before heading down to Foreshore Road for the day's entertainment. Approximately eleven thirty am on the beach, the town Mayor of Scarborough would kick off the annual Fishermen v Fireman football match. The football match had continued from that first sea disaster, in the days of the old steam trawlers. By now the towns steam trawlers were extinct, but all the players, the referee included, were still recruited from within the local fishing industry. There were no strict rules, and no limits on size or age. The Fishermen wore white shirts, black tailed coats, and black top hats. The Firemen (whom, at one time stoked the boilers on the old steam trawlers) wore the same clothes but in red. Because it was for charity the match was played in a comic style. At half time after a few pints of beer, or glasses of spirits were consumed by both sides, across the road in the 'Lord Nelson' pub, which resulted to much more fun in the second half. Rules were completely ignored, players were tripped, sat upon or even thrown into the sea, including the referee, so by the time the final whistle was blown some of the players might be bruised, soaking wet, or tipsy, but no one really bothered or cared about the score, because everyone had a great time, spectators and players alike, plus the charity collections swelled. With the ending of the football match everyone made for the pubs to continue the celebrations. After the pubs had closed there was usually parties still going strong in some of the bottom end homes. Unsurprisingly, due to acute hangovers, not many people reported for work the following day.

Though not like the more outlandish and daring fashions in London, Scarborough's youth still followed the trends. A young man or woman's dress sense did not really exist in the previous generations, they were just similar version of their mothers or fathers dress code, even in some cases young men wearing a flat hat, and smoking a pipe. Now, suits for young men were not just for special occasions, and they were far more varied and different in style from the previous generations. Burtons and John Collier were popular tailors for the young men, where you could be measured and fitted for a suit in less than four weeks, all to your own style, colours and patterns. The trousers we insisted must be narrowed legged, and you could buy your suit on the hire purchase, so most of the youths had a number of suits. Waist coats, once considered old fashioned, became popular once more, but now your waist coat and suit jacket linings could be made in a range of patterns and bright colours. Winkle pickers and Italian shaped shoes, which only a short time ago were popular; had defiantly gone out of fashion. Chelsea boots were now the vogue. The boots came up to your ankles, with elasticised sides, and thick squared toes with high flat Cuban heels. White dress shirts were still popular although other colours were now being worn, but ties had to be pencil slim, while casual jackets and trousers were varied in both style and colours. The rules of fashion? There were no rules, you wore what you wanted to wear. At the time smoking cigarettes was the cool thing to do, after all, even in the movies. the stars including the females, always had the obliging cigarette dangling in their fingers, which was now highlighted by the very fashion-conscious recording artists. In Scarborough the girls and young women were more focused and daring than the men, and they matched their southern counter parts in both fashion and style. Teenagers now had not only the money to spend, but a voice to be heard, and they were becoming more political aware than their parents had been before. As I have already stated the music was wide and varied, but if you liked the more rock orientated or progressive type of music, a few years later a new club opened in St Nicolas Street called 'The 'Penthouse'. The Penthouse was to achieve cult status in the Scarborough music venues, and many of the bands and artists who appeared at The Penthouse although virtually unknown at the time went on to acquire worldwide recognition, future stars such as David Bowie, Free, Mark Bolen, The Manfred Mann Free Band, Derek and the Dominoes, (fronted by Eric Clapton) and also a group fronted by a local man Alan Palmer, who later would change his name to Robert Palmer, and achieve near cult status. For the first time young people had money to spend and were a force to be recognised. All this demand for the new music had not gone unnoticed by the business sector, and pubs were now installing juke boxes with all the latest hit records, and a few of the larger pubs were even booking local groups at the weekends to entertain their cliental. Working men's and other social clubs, were also booking not just local groups but also groups from other towns. I divided most of my spare time to many of the venues and discothèques that I have mentioned, but my favourite, perhaps because it was the first one, was 'The Scene', and it was at the Scene that I first met Irena, my future wife. So, within the space of six years Scarborough had diverted from a dirge of fashion, music, and entertainment, to a lively, vibrant, and outward looking East Coast town. The 'Sixties' is regarded as the decade of free love and drugs, well maybe in London. But it did not reach as far as Scarborough that I can recall. The only drugs that I can remember is music, and beer. There is a saying 'If you can remember the sixties you weren't there.'

Well I can remember the sixties, and I can assure you that I WAS THERE.

CHAPTER 11

POETIC AWAKENING

I met Irena one Friday night at The Scene discothèque, and we made a date to meet again. From there our romance blossomed, and on the 21st of September 1968 we were married. In the following years we had two daughters Joanna and Sharon, I was buying my own house, and work was plentiful in the building trade. I was happy to be employed on a number of small and large extensions, also on the construction of new major buildings in and around the Scarborough area. The following twenty-one years were eventful and happy, except for the sudden death at sixty-three years of age, of my dad in 1973, which was a terrible loss to the family, and myself in particular. For the last few years dad and I had overcome the generation gap; and we had become to understand each other's attitude to life. Dad, like most of his generation had toiled long and hard with little reward for most of his life, and then came the outbreak of the Second World War. Dad was one of the first to volunteer in the army, and he was awarded medals for his service in Italy, Malta, and North Africa. After the war he left the army as a Sergeant in the Royal Artillery. Dad was abroad for five years yet he rarely spoke of his war years, but he always regarded himself as fortunate to have survived the war physically, however he had seen many good men killed or maimed, and he had also witnessed a lot of destruction, and poverty. Back home dad settled back into more years of toil, but ended his working life contented, as the caretaker of the local Catholic School. Dad held a hope that future generations would benefit from the huge social changes that were made after the war. I had always been aware of dad's aspirations and I had sworn to myself that after serving my apprenticeship I would work hard and honestly for my family, but demand fair financial rewards for my work, and would not toe down to unfairness and exploitation.

It was then 1990, and the following incident that occurred was to have a profound effect on my future life. Our house was situated in Trafalgar Road a busy terraced road. The large house next door had been converted into four holiday flats, but in the winter months the flats were rented out on a temporary basis until the following Spring, so we were accustomed to different people coming and going all through the year. It was early evening one Friday night in March, I had just entered the lounge, and Irena had just drawn the lounge curtains before Sharon and herself settled down to an evening with the television. Suddenly there was a huge explosion and the curtains lit up in a blinding orange and red flash. Alarmed, I rushed to the front door thinking that perhaps my car, or some other car had exploded. On opening the front door I was horrified to see huge tongues of flames shooting out from the now windowless ground floor flat next door. The flames were so fierce that they had reached nearly halfway across to the other side of the road. I shouted to Irena to call the fire brigade, and then, running across the road, dodging the flames and the blown out front door of the house, I ran up to the blazing doorway. For a few seconds I stared in horror at the roaring fire, alongside James, a neighbour who had just joined me. Flames were shooting out of the openings of the ground floor flat, while the whole of the hallway of the house and staircase were ablaze in a searing crackling flame. To our alarm, in the middle of the hallway, we saw staggering, a screaming figure completely immersed in flames. Without conferring with each other, James and I simultaneously dashed into the inferno together. The heat in the hallway was tremendous, and the smoke filled our mouths and noses, making breathing extremely difficult. The figure was staggering blindly around the hallway making pitiful screeching noises, while all around us small explosions were erupting (those small explosions we were to learn later were aerosol cans expanding with the intense heat) the heat became unbearable making James and I stagger back to the doorway, gulping in some fresh clean air. As we turned round we saw that the figure had now collapsed onto the floor. I quickly removed my thick woollen jumper, and wrapping it around my head, I entered the hallway once more. James, having removed his own jumper, wrapped it around his head and followed. The blazing figure was now motionless, but moaning pityingly. The heat was intense, so grabbing the figure under its arms between us, James and I began dragging it slowly to the doorway, and then onto the outside footpath. After beating out the flames on the figure we realised that it was that of a young man who was now groaning softly, with smoke drifting from his badly burnt clothes, in the process some of his scorched skin had clung to my hands. The explosion, and everything that had occurred seemed to be an age, yet it was only a matter of minutes before a fire engine tore down the street and screeched to a halt outside the blazing house. The fire crew quickly streamed into a calm and organised action, while an emergency doctor also arrived at the same time. The doctor quickly jumped out of his car, and case in hand he dashed over to us and began treating the still smouldering man. The rest of that night became a shadowed blur, I can only recall the doctor bandaging my blistered hands, and then answering some questions to a fire officer and a detective. The following day news of the drama had spread across the town, and the phone kept ringing constantly as friends and relations enquired about my own welfare, while the detective questioned me once more in detail. Reporters from two local newspapers also wanted to interview me, James was also experiencing the same procedures. The next night the Scarborough Evening News reported the incident. The young man was named as Anthony Hargreaves 24 years of age He had been taken to Pinderfields Hospital burns unit in Wakefield, and he was in a critical condition, with 70% burns to his body. Although the enormity of the incident had not yet sunk in, and my hands were still sore, I returned to work on the Monday morning, and although the incident was mentioned I was relieved that not a lot of questions were asked. Three days later, sadly Anthony, never regained conciseness and died in Wakefield Hospital. Thankfully after Anthony's death the media coverage of the tragedy began to receded, but for me the nightmares had only just begun. I will not go into more detail of the horrors that James and I witnessed that night, because only someone who experienced such a situation can truly understand completely the turmoil that we were going through. Some night in bed, I would relive that night's horror in detail, but even more terrifying. I would also hear once again those animal-like screams of agony, and other nights I would suddenly jolt up sweating, and shake my hands desperately trying to rid myself of the scorched skin that I imagined was dangling from my hands. From the outside I seemed my usual happy self but inside, my mind was in turmoil, unfortunately Irena and Sharon who were at the time the closest to me received the butt of my frustrations. Around six weeks later an inquest of that night's tragedy took place. But because Anthony had never regained conciseness the police were never able to clarify the actual motive. However because of the findings, and the careful piecing together of

172

the facts by both the police and the fire brigade, the following report was concluded.

Anthony was living with his girlfriend in the winter let flat. He had a slight mental disorder and at times a violent temper, and on a number of occasions he had hit his pregnant girlfriend. Anthony, to his credit had accepted his condition and on a voluntary basis he was admitted to a special unit of a nearby hospital. While he was in the unit, his girlfriend had packed her personal belongings and moved away. The next day Anthony discharged himself from the hospital, but when he arrived back at the flat, realising that his girlfriend had left him, he went to a nearby petrol station and purchased a plastic petrol can, and filled it with petrol, before returning back to the flat. He then began to pour the petrol around the flat, and in the process splashing himself with the petrol. Realising he had nothing to light the fire with, he went to the corner shop and purchased a box of matches, he then returned back to the flat. However, in his absence lethal petrol fumes had built up, and as he struck a match the flat, and himself exploded into fire. Because of his confused state of mind and the medication that he was taking at the time, it was not known if Anthony intended to end his own life, or if he was even actually aware of his actions, but unfortunately we will never know. The owner of the property Margaret, lived in the background floor flat, and thankfully she escaped unharmed, as did a man, the only other resident at the time who thankfully was not in his flat at the time of the fire. Although the inquest brought the incident to a satisfactory conclusion, for me the turmoil still continued. One Saturday morning a number of weeks after the inquest, Irena and myself were at home when Irena, after answering the front door bell, re-entered the lounge with the station officer of the Scarborough Fire Brigade. After a polite greeting the Officer informed me that James and I were going to be given an award for outstanding bravery. He also added that it was the fire services highest bravery award for civilians, and that very few had been issued in the last ten years. Far from being proud, I was annoyed and angry, and denied being a hero, and to the fire officer's amazement I refused the award. The officer slightly confused, asked me if everything was alright, but when I assured him that it was, Irena looked first at the fire officer then myself, and said softly.

"Terry it isn't, as well you know, tell him, please?"

The officer looked at me for a few seconds, and then he said in a firm but polite tone.

"Look Terry, don't take this the wrong way but I think that you really do need some professional help, especially if you are having difficulties coping."

I was outraged at his suggestion but before I could reply the officer seeing my anger, continued more forcefully.

"Terry, as firemen we see sights that you can never even imagine, and although we are trained to deal with these tragedies, even we professionals sometimes are affected by what we see. So for us to deal with these sights sometimes we ourselves need counselling. What you and James experienced that night was indeed horrifying, and for you both to walk away from that experience and not be affected by it is nigh imposable."

As the Officer rose he put a card on the coffee table and then he looked at me and added.

"I'll leave this number for you Terry. Obviously whether you use it or not is entirely up to you. But Terry, I strongly advise you to do so."

The fire officer's strong but well-meant words jolted me, and made me think. A few days later I eventually succumbed, and I made an appointment, and received the counselling that I badly needed.

I have to admit that I was very sceptical at first, however after only that first meeting with the counsellor I literary poured out all my pent-up feelings. I cannot recall the man's name, or most of his words, except for something that he had remarked.

"Terry, because Anthony had died, and although you could not prevent his death, you have taken on some of his own guilt". The counsellor suggested that I should try and write down on paper my thoughts of that fateful night, which might help to bleed my mind. Back home that night, I did write about what had occurred, but for some strange unknown reason I wrote the words in a poetic way, and not only did writing of the words ease my mind a little, but I found that I enjoyed the poetic creativity. From then on I wrote a number of poems on varying subjects, although at first they were somewhat garbled, and very amateurish, eventually the writing of poetry slowly helped to unblock my mind. Two months later at The Scarborough Fire Station I, along with James received our awards from the Yorkshire County Chief Fire officer. It was about only the third time that James and I had been in contact since that fateful night of the fire, although we lived only two doors away from each other. I think we both felt the same way about that night, and did not want to relive it again. James was in the army at the time and he had been in action in the Falklands, but he told me that he had not witnessed anything like that before. If James received any counselling like me I don't know, but after the fire he began to drink heavily. Not long after receiving the award, James and his wife sold their house and moved away from Scarborough, I sincerely hope that James did not become a victim of a tortured mind.

I never considered myself to be a hero at the time; and I still feel the same way today. I think that is the feeling of most people involved in a similar situation as myself, especially in the armed forces. However, in the following years the love of writing poetry not only brought me personal pleasure and rewards, but it also gave me a cushion for the sorrows that were to follow. That same year Francis began to have serious breathing problems due to the tuberculosis that she had contacted in her younger years. After many months in and out of hospital, Francis finally passed away just two days before Christmas 1990. In the next three years, another three family deaths were to occur. Mum, who unfortunately was admitted to a nursing home with dementia some months before Francis's illness, also died the following year of a heart attack. Only a few months later Teresa's husband Arthur, collapsed and died also of a heart attack. Meanwhile Ted, divorced from his wife had been complaining of stomach pains which had persisted, and after a number of visits to the doctor, and a test at the Scarborough hospital, Ted was diagnosed with cancer of the pancreas, which was spreading rapidly. Refusing any treatment apart from pain killers, Ted declared that, 'Rather than have only a few more years of life left; consisting of constant pain, pills and therapy I am prepared to let the cancer run its course.'

Ted only lived another few months, he was divorced now, but his 16 year old son Paul and himself never saw eye to eye, so as Ted lived on his own I would visit him regularly. To see anyone daily ravaged to something like a skeleton by that ruthless disease is horrific. Thankfully, though a loss, Ted passed away in Scarborough hospital. For a few years before his death Ted and I had become close, none more so than in his final weeks. Many times since Ted has passed away; I have been grateful that I was at his side when he needed somebody, and I always advise people to bear no grudges to anybody, especially if they are related, for life is too short to have vendettas and anger.

Although it might seem that those years were full of doom and sorrow it was certainly not the case. Joanna met, and then married, a local boy, Steve Heritage, who was serving in the Royal Navy. For a while they lived in Scarborough where to our delight our first grandchild Nicole was born. Then three years later a son, Jamie followed. Steve, along with Joanna and their family, were then stationed to Gosport near Portsmouth. Also to our surprise Sharon, always the home bird moved with a friend to live Sunderland. However, for myself the memory of that fire still remained, but it was slowly receding, due to my writing poetry, and also music and reading. From my early scrabbled beginnings of poetry I began to mould and structure my words, and I also enjoyed reading other people's poetry. Success followed, and I had many poems published in newspapers, magazines and poetry books. Being in the building trade I fully expected to be the butt of many jokes and comments, which did occur, however it was all done in a light-hearted manner, in fact I received a lot of nice comments and encouragement from all quarters. In 1996 Steve, with Joanna and their young family had been posted to Gibraltar for three years, and both of them soon fell in love with the country. Irena and I had been to visit them in Gibraltar a number of times, and we also liked not only the climate, but the way of life in Gibraltar. Sharon, with her friend was still enjoying her time in Sunderland. With only five years left on my mortgage I was considering to paying it off completely, so it seemed that everyone in the family were content and settled. However the road of life has many turnings, because the following years were to bring to me a change of life, filled with both happiness and misfortune.

CHAPTER 12

THE ROCK.

I had now settled into a happy married family life. I was self-employed and work was plenty. I worked hard during the week earning a good wage, but if possible, I kept the weekends free. Joanna and Sharon had now both moved away with lives of their own to lead, and I looked forward to my Friday and Saturday nights, a steady drink, lots of laugher with friends, and usually on one of the nights go out on my own to watch and listen to any live music (defiantly not Karaoke) Irena worked part time at the local Morrison's supermarket, and occasionally we would go out for a meal, or socialise with friends. Joanna and her family, now that Steve's posting in Gibraltar was over, had been posted back to Gosport. Many months previous Sharon was restless at Sunderland, so at Joanna's insistence Sharon had moved to join her sister at Gibraltar. However when Steve and Joanna returned back to the U.K Sharon now having made friends, and liking the Gibraltar way of life had decided to stay. I was still writing and enjoying my poetry, but the horrors of the fire although somewhat diminished, still existed at the back of my mind. One night in the early spring of 2000, Irena and I were talking about the happy times we had shared with Joanna and her family and also Sharon, on our holidays in Gibraltar, when out of the blue Irena remarked.

"Why don't we move to Gibraltar?"

To say I was shocked was an understatement because Irena and I were now well into our middle age and although I was a skilled tradesman I knew very little of the building trade in Gibraltar or even of its existence, and at

179

my age the prospect to retrain into another occupation was not appealing. Also if we uprooted, what if the move proved disastrous both financially and personally. However as Irena pointed out, we could rent out our house for a six month period while we were in Gibraltar, and the rent for the house would cover the mortgage, and if the worst happened at least we would still have a home back in Scarborough to come back too. For a few days I thought about the proposal, then I really began to warm to the idea, but the final clinch for me was the thought that perhaps the move would give me something positive to focus on and hopefully eliminate the horrors of the fire that still troubled me. The more we discussed and worked to achieve the move; the more enthusiastic I became. Come August 20000 everything was in order. The house, fully furnished was rented out for an initial six months by a local estate agent. All my tax and N.H.S. stamps were brought up to date, and our personal items were stored in a friend's house. Finally after every little detail of our departure had been settled, a new life beckoned.

Sharon was renting a flat in Gibraltar at the time, so at first it was planned that we would stay with her for a short while to give Irena and myself some time to look for a furnished flat for ourselves; and hopefully employment for us both. We had only taken a large suitcase each, containing clothes and a few vital necessities, however we were both determined to make a go of our new life. We had intended to spend the first week as a holiday but as Sharon was working full time and Irena and I were both eager to find a place of our own, coupled with the fact that I wanted to find employment as soon as possible, we began in earnest in our quests the following day. While Irena toured the local estate agents for a possible furnished flat, I walked around the various building sites looking for employment.

To my dismay two points that I discovered within the first hour, was that apart from the buildings that had been built in brick by the armed forces, the vast majority of the other new buildings were constructed in concrete blocks and then coated by a sand and cement facing, which to me possessed no real skill., and although Gibraltar was part of the United Kingdom and the Gibraltarians classed themselves as British citizens, the dominant language was Spanish. However after much searching I came across a joiner on a building site who originated from Leeds but he was now a resident in Spain, I explained about my trade, and the fact that I was seeking self-employment, or even to be employed. The joiner, who himself was self-employed had resided in Spain for ten years and he was fluent in the Spanish language, which he insisted was vital to any work in Spain. However he told me of a building firm based in Gibraltar owned by two British tradesmen, John Temple and Phil Norton, both, whom he insisted were strict but knowledgeable construction workers, and they kept everything above board. After directions I arrived at the building company's office, where, in the front yard, inspecting an old concrete mixer, I came across a middle aged, tall, well-built man sporting a small moustache, and wearing a white tee-shirt and white shorts. After asking for either of the owners, the man looked at me indifferently and answered that he was John Temple. I explained that I was a bricklayer and looking for work, John Temple glared at me and snarled.

"Are you sure you're a bricklayer. You're not a b------ carpet salesman, a window cleaner or something like that, are you?"

For a few seconds I was taken aback by his brusque manner, so thinking he was being sarcastic I snapped back.

"No, like I said I'm a bricklayer, and a time served bricklayer, not a cowboy."

John never flinched at my response but he replied in a more civilised manner.

"Well, I'm sorry that I was a bit off hand. But I've got to ask because we get all sorts of odd balls coming to Gib saying they are this and that, yet they turn out to be right proper dumb heads, and they don't know nothing about the building trade."

Before I could reply, John looked at my angry face, and replied abruptly.

"Okay, I'll give you a start, come here Monday morning at eight o'clock sharp."

He paused, and added

"I'll give you a week's trial to see if you're any good."

Staring directly back at him I replied.

"Fine, and I'll give you a week's trial to see if your firm is any good."

That would not be the first time I would cross swords with John Temple, and I would not be the only one in his line of fire. Even top officials were victims to John's erratic moods. But over the years I found that John, like his partner Phil Norton were both direct, but honest and helpful employers. John and Phil were also very knowledgeable men, and over a period of time we became good friends. Irena and I, to our dismay found that the price of property to buy or rent in Gibraltar was high, and because of the rapid developments over the last two years prices had nearly doubled, however we did manage to find a reasonably priced, furnished one bedroom flat near the town centre.

That first year in Gibraltar was hard in many ways because Irena and I were virtually starting all over again. Thankfully the rent from our Scarborough property paid the mortgage on the house, and although we both had employment and we could afford the rent for the flat in Gibraltar, but with only our savings to fall back on it meant that we had to be careful. Luckily Irena had found employment with Safeway's supermarket (later to be Morrison's) so because money was tight, we never bothered with a television set for that first year. However, with the pleasant climate, most of our spare time we spent walking around, and discovering the older and historic Gibraltar, and marvelled at the beauty of the country. However, just a few years later that same picturesque landscape that we then enjoyed, would be dominated by huge concrete and glass constructions, but, seeing that I had in a small way helped to construct the same constructions I could not really complain. In the following two years we had to return back to Scarborough twice to sort out the mess left by two different uncaring tenants, by which time; fed up with renting our house to ungrateful strangers, and because we both agreed that we wanted to remain in Gibraltar, we put the house in Scarborough up for sale. Gradually we began to make a pleasant social life, making many friends among the cross section of society in Gibraltar. About a hundred metres from our flat was Casements Square, or Casements, as they are called locally. They were first constructed many years ago to serve as a military prison before later being converted into living accommodation for the many Moroccans who came over to work and live in Gibraltar, but the buildings had deteriorated since those days. However just before we arrived in Gibraltar, the square and the buildings had been updated and modernised into a series of pleasant restaurants, bars, and various tourist shops. For me the 'Lord Nelson Bar' was the place that I frequented on Saturday nights, simply because of its abundance of excellent musicians, and lovers of live music. The main attraction obviously was the live music, appreciated by its regular clientele, which was a cross section of Gibraltar society. One particular regular was Enrico. Enrico was born in Gibraltar, however when he was younger, with his parents and sister he had moved to the U.K. and lived in London for a number of years. Enrico eventually returned back to Gibraltar and he was now serving in the Gibraltar Police force. Enrico actually started his police career in London and he also was a live music lover, and like myself he had become part of the regular cliental that used the Lord Nelson at the weekends. Besides the music we all enjoyed a great sense of humour, and Enrico told us of a number of amusing incidents and situations when he first began his career in the London police force, one of which I will now retell.

The Police station where Enrico served was friendly and had a great comradeship, plus a great humour. Whenever a person after training, first began as a constable, as a prank the rookie would be taken to the local morgue. Because it was explained that it was a crucial element in the job that the rookie should see for themselves a real corpse. However, some minutes before the rookie was escorted to the morgue, another police officer would slip into a drawer fully clothed, and his mates would whiten his face slightly, they then covered him over with a sheet and closed the drawer before concealing themselves in an adjoining room. The joke being that, when the drawer was pulled out and the corpse's face uncovered, the corpse would suddenly rise up and shout 'boo'.

Thus, the poor rookie would reel back in shock, which always guaranteed laughter. But one day unbeknown to the officer who had gleefully volunteered to be the corpse, two other colleagues had crept into the morgue only minutes earlier, and one of them, well wrapped up because of the cold, had slipped into the adjoining drawer next to the pretended corpse. On time the unsuspecting officer crept into the next drawer, gleefully anticipating the shocked reaction of the rookie police officer A few seconds later a deep voice boomed in the pitch blackness,

"I don't know about you mate, but I'm f-------- freezing in here."

Enrico said that the screaming and banging of the so-called corpse was hilarious,

Over the next few years I spent many happy hours in The Lord Nelson, and made many friends both British and Gibraltarian, old, and young. The standard of musicians, and singers in Gibraltar were excellent, and put to shame the present load of Karaoke type rubbish now thrust upon to our television screens. Gibraltar was expanding all the time, not just in the constructions, but also in the cost of housing. Gibraltar shares its border with Spain, and just across the border is the Spanish town of La Linea, where the cost of living, and property were far more cheaper than in Gibraltar, so many British, and even Gibraltarians, had either rented or bought property in La Linea, because commuting across the border to Gibraltar was then fairly easy, so with our house in Scarborough still on the market it was a course of action Irena and myself had decided to follow. At first, we rented a three-bed roomed flat close to La Linea beach on the ninth floor with a balcony and a panoramic view of both Gibraltar and the La Linea beaches, plus on a fine day the coast of Africa could be seen shimmering in the distance. In the process of moving we had sold our house and the furniture in Scarborough, so transporting our personal belongings over, we relocated to our new flat in La Linea. However, because of the slump in the English property market at the time we had received far less for the house than we had anticipated, but to compensate for our disappointment Joanna's husband Steve, had requested for another overseas posting, and to their, and our surprise and great delight, Steve had been posted back to Gibraltar, which meant that the family were reunited once again. The weekends in the summer months we spent playing on the beach, or swimming in the sea with Sharon, Joanna and Steve, and of course our grandchildren Nicole and Jamie. Another of our favourite pastimes was, relaxing in the bars and idyllic surroundings of Gibraltar's Marina Bay. The property boom in Gibraltar had now spread to Spain, and the price of property had risen sharply. Anxious to buy a property while we could afford the mortgage, we put most of the money we had made on the house in Scarborough down as a deposit on a two-bed roomed flat on the second floor in the centre of La Linea, which was a case of out of one hand into another. However, we were as happy as we had ever been, and Joanna and her family were now settled in a newly built naval family accommodation in Gibraltar. Sharon who was working in a bar in Casement Square had also moved into a rented flat in La Linea only a ten minutes' walk from our own flat, so we were all settled in our new accommodations and employments.

To say that the building trade was different to the U.K. was an understatement, as I have already mentioned a lot of the buildings were built in concrete blocks, not just ordinary concrete blocks but heavy monstrous concrete blocks weighing nearly five kilo's each, and although I was employed as a bricklayer, like everybody else on the firm I was expected to turn my hand to anything that was required. Being able to do bricklaying, stonework, plastering, and tiling was a great advantage, although I also learnt from John and Phil, a number jobs in civil engineering such as concreting, steel fixing, kerb laying, and laying brick sets around buildings and roads, and numerous other building works, and if required, even at times painting and labouring. The only disappointment being that the work was not of the standard I was accustomed too, also the rate of pay compared to the U.K. was much lower, but our reason for moving to Gibraltar was not materialistic. The firm I worked for employed a nucleus of about thirty men most of whom were British, but also a few Gibraltarians, although like the building trade in the U.K. more men were recruited according to the work load. The standard of work in Gibraltar done by some of the building firms were at times appalling, and most of the Clerk of Works or what you might call building inspectors at the time were Gibraltarians, and unlike their British counterparts they had very little building experience, so there appeared to be a lot of work done; that was well below the British standard. A common practice at that time in most Gibraltar employment, no matter what qualifications or experience a person might possess, a Gibraltarian was always the first choice. Although it seemed anything goes, and with little restrictions in the building trade, John Temple and Paul Norton standards were of the highest quality, and their contracts were usually completed to schedule, hence their firm was always in demand. Also like in the U.K, the building trade employed a lot of a casual workers, with an assortment of different characters drifting in and out of the trade, the majority were hard working and honest but some, although honest and hardworking still provoked humour or comical situations. I will mention just a few of the many instances among the many I encountered while working in Gibraltar.

There was a drink culture in Gibraltar, not surprising really when you think that from April until October the sun shines constantly, and In July and August particular the heat becomes almost unbearable, especially if like me you worked in the building trade and your work is mostly conducted on the outside. One of the easiest ways to get along the narrow roads in Gibraltar and across the Spanish border is on a motor bike or motor scooter, as these are the most favoured modes of transport. While Irena used our car I had bought a motor scooter, and although apprehensive at first I found that riding a scooter was far more exhilarating and relaxing than the confines of a car. Nearly every night in the summer months after finishing work, and wearing just a tee shirt and shorts, I would cross the border on my scooter, with the thought of that ice cool can of beer waiting for me in the fridge. Although I liked my beer, I was not a big drinker unlike some in Gibraltar.

Mickey had been resident in Gibraltar for about six years, originally from London, he was small in height and build, with short cropped hair. Mickey was a bricklayer by trade and he was well known for liking his drink, however Mickey was also a hard worker; and a good bricklayer, and good tradesmen were hard to find in Gibraltar, so his fondness for a drink was often overlooked. One very wet and windy autumn mid-afternoon Mickey had got a calling for a drink, so he made for his favourite bar down on the Marina. By teatime Mickey was now very inebriated, and he was stood talking and swaying at the bar with a number of his friends who had just finished their own days' work. Among them was Dave a joiner, and Mario, a young Gibraltarian labourer who was usually very upbeat, however that day the conversation had started to get a little morbid, as a sorrowful Mario began telling the men gathered around the bar of how much he missed his Uncle Johan, whom he had lived with for most of his life, but Johan unfortunately had died exactly a year ago.

Dave, fed up with Mario's morbid mood, remarked rather abruptly.

"Well everybody's got to go sometime Mario you've just got to accept it, like everybody else does."

Mario bemoaned,

"Yeah yeah, I know a-that Dave, but I not carried out uncle Johan's last wish."

Mickey and Dave exchanged glances. So Mickey, bleary eyed, looked at Mario, and put down his half empty glass on the bar.

"So what was your uncle Johan's last wish then Mario?"

"My Uncle Johan, you understand, he not a Catholic so he wanna be cremated, and he say when he die that I gotta scatter his ashes at sea."

Dave, looking bemused asked.

"So! Did you scatter his ashes then?"

"No, that's just it Dave, his ashes are still in the urn. Because after the funeral I put the urn on top of my wardrobe and forgot them until today, so they still there."

A bemused Dave looked at Mario, and grinned

"What! Do you mean to say that the urn with your Uncle Johan's ashes is still on the top of your f-----wardrobe?"

Mario looking crestfallen simply nodded. However Mickey lifted up his glass and with one swift drink he gulped the beer down his throat, then swaying unsteadily he stared with wide eyes at Mario. and slurred.

"Hey Mario, you only live a few minutes away from here don't you?"

Mario looking perplexed simply nodded.

"Good, well you go and get the urn from the wardrobe, and together we'll both go and scatter his ashes at the end of the Marina right now, okay?"

But Dave yelled,

"You what! Have you seen the f------ weather out there Mickey, you'll both get blown away you daft b--------"

However Mario, now beaming with delight, was already walking out of the bar door.

Dave and a few other men remonstrated unsuccessfully with a now a very inebriated Mickey. But, only few minutes later Mario, still grinning, stepped back into the bar, staggering with the urn clutched in his hands. Mickey walked over to join Mario, and although the rain had ceased, the wind was still blowing hard and wild. Dave looked at the rest of us reluctantly, and shaking his head accompanied Mickey and Mario out onto the wind-swept Marina. Ten minutes later the outside door to the bar swung open and a laughing Dave, and a downcast Mario entered the bar. Dave laughing addressed the other men in the bar.

"Aw man, what a b------- laugh. I followed those two drunken idiots; making sure that I was close behind them, because with the wind blowing and the state that they both were in I was scared in case something might happen to them. By the time we had got to the end of the Marina the wind was really blowing strong. Anyway, Mario took off the lid of the urn and gingerly held out the urn over the water, but he got right weepy, so Mickey just snatched the urn off Mario and quickly

emptied the ashes out of the urn himself but......"

Dave began to laugh once more while holding onto the bar counter. The other men smiling, looked on in anticipation, until impatiently one of the men asked sharply.

"Well come on Dave don`t keep us in suspense, tell us then what the hell happened?"

Dave braced himself before he replied.

"Well the wind only blew the f-------- ashes back all over Mickey didn't it?"

As everybody burst out laughing, the bar door suddenly swung open, and Mickey staggered in to the bar, with the front of his coat and his face covered in a grey ash. The laughter calmed down as Mickey staggered over to a table, slumped into a chair and growled

"It's like the b----- Klondike out there, quick, somebody get me a pint."

As Mickey laid back into his chair looking somewhat nonplussed, with only his lips and the white of his eyes showing through the grey ash, a voice shouted out.

"Hey Mickey! I see you've brought uncle Johan back with you does he want a pint as well."

Mickey and myself, and Sean another friend and bricklayer, were involved in another hilarious situation also involving Mario. The three of us were on a scaffold, building a concrete block wall in a large warehouse; on an industrial site. The internal wall was going to be painted so the finish of the blocks had to be neat and tidy that meant that any cut blocks also had to be decently cut. To cut the monstrous block, a portable concrete cutter had been hired, and Mario had been given the task to cut the blocks to any size that was required by the bricklayers. Mickey had no patience with anybody he regarded as a buffoon, unfortunately Mario came into that reckoning. Mickey bemoaned the fact that Mario 'was not all there', so he would not entertain Mario. Mario however, to his credit was good natured, and never seemed to care about Mickey's assumption of him, so he was always in a smiling, pleasant mood. One morning Mario asked if we needed any blocks cutting,

Sean shook his head and said no, Mickey completely ignored Mario, but I asked Mario to cut five pieces of blocks at 100 mm each. Five minutes later Mario climbed the ladder to the top of the scaffold, and gave me one cut block, and grinning he said.

"That's one at 100mm`s, now you want four more, no Terry

(Gibraltarians always seem to end a sentence with the question no) I nodded, but I also advised Mario that to save many journeys it would be better cut them, and then bring to them all up the scaffold in the same trip. Mario still grinning, nodded in agreement before descending the ladder. Five minutes later Mario, to Sean's and my amusement, climbed up the ladder once more and gave me another cut block, then grinning once more he remarked.

"That another one at 100 metres. Three more Terry, no?"

Instead of repeating my earlier suggestion I simply nodded, Sean smiled, however Mickey at the other end of the scaffold looked at me sadly, and shook his head as if to say 'I told you so'. About ten minutes after climbing the ladder three more times with my cut blocks Mario shouted up from the ground level.

"Hey Sean, Mickey, you now wanna any cuts now?"

Sean again shook his head and said no, but to my surprise Mickey shouted back.

"Yea Mario, will you cut me a block in half."

Mickey turned to a surprised Sean and myself, shrugged his shoulders and commented.

"Surely, even he can't get that b------ wrong."

However, a few minutes later Mario shouted up from the ground.

"Hey Mickey, which you wanta first, the big half or the little half?"

In an earlier chapter I said how much I detested bullies, and that is the same with nastiness and racialism, all of which I detest, but as I have also stated bullies will always get their come-uppance as the following incident shows. The firm that I worked for, as well as having their own contracts,

and because of their reliability and standard of work, they were often in demand from the other

Gibraltar building firms to hire out some of the company's work force. Sean and I, along with some of the other workmen had been hired out to a large block of flats that were under construction by the largest building firm in Gibraltar. Louie, a Gibraltarian was the manager in charge of the site, Louie, besides being a honest and pleasant man was also very knowledgeable of the construction trade, and he possessed a friendly nature. However, another English man Ronnie, who also worked for the same Gibraltar firm, had no actually trade, but somehow he had wormed himself in to be Louie's unofficial second in command. Ronnie was a ginger haired, loud and overbearing, arrogant man, and a typical bully, but not to those who would stand their ground. The Gibraltar firm also employed a number of Moroccan labourers, whom by their own nature were submissive, hardworking, friendly, and very honest people, a sure target for the bombastic Ronnie. One day a large consignment of rough heavy timber needed to be unloaded from a lorry, Ronnie had taken it upon himself to be in charge of the unloading, and he had issued pairs of work gloves to the labourers, consisting of two Spanish, and two Moroccans, with the strict instructions that they should look after the gloves. Even though the men worked hard and diligently Ronnie clapping his own gloved hands, though not actually working himself, bawled and shouted abuse like a German camp commander. Eventually when the lorry was unloaded Ronnie nastily ordered the men to return back to their previous jobs, and then with his chest puffed out, Ronnie marched to the site office to reassure Louie that the task had been completed. However he had left behind his work gloves at the side of the road where Sean and I were working. Sean picked up the gloves, winked at me, and hid them under a stack of concrete blocks. A little while later Ronnie came marching directly towards us, and asked if we had seen his gloves, which he was certain he had left near to where Sean and I were working. We both growled back an abusive answer. Ronnie was fuming that we had dismissed him so negatively, but he was also aware that to pursue the matter with Sean and myself any further was useless. However he furiously demanded the same question to everybody else who were in the vicinity. At that precise moment Mohamed and Haemal the two Moroccan workers, who had helped unload the lorry, came walking down the road each pushing a wheel barrow, stacked with mixed pieces of scrap wood. Ronnie was now in an even fouler mood and he pounced onto the unsuspecting Moroccans.

"Hey! Have you F------- wogs seen my gloves?"

The Moroccans, terrified at Ronnie's violent mood; shook their heads in denial. However their response seemed to fuel Ronnie's temper even more and with a roar he marched up to them upturned their barrows and began searching among the wood, to see if his gloves had been hidden amongst them. Suddenly Ronnie stopped, and looking at Mohamed`s hands he snarled.

"Hey! Those are my f------- gloves, give me them back to me now you thieving wog.."

Mohamed's eyes widened in fright.

"No, no Mr Ronnie you wrong, I keep them on all the time from when you give me them."

However Ronnie was in no mood for denial.

"You f------- thieving wog they're mine, give me them back now."

Ronnie lunged at Mohamed. However Mohamed in one foul swoop; scooped up a short thick piece of wood and slammed it into Ronnie's snarling face. Ronnie dropped to the ground like a felled tree, with blood spouting from his nose and face. Slowly he put a hand to his face, jumped up, and began running down the road, with blood streaming through his hand, and to jeers and hoops of delight from all around the site, he screamed.

"He hit me, he hit me, the b------ wog hit me..."

The outcome after Louie investigated the incident? Far from disciplining the two Moroccans, Louie gave a weeks' notice to Ronnie for abusive and nasty behaviour, but he also gave the two Moroccans, Mohamed and Haemal, some extra money for that week, which proves a saying I have always believed. 'What goes around, comes around'

Sean had lived and worked in Gibraltar for over thirty years, he was a well-known character and liked by most people. Sean besides being a good worker and bricklayer, was also a knowledgeable person, and although a bit of a maverick he was held in high regard by the management. Sean was a non-smoker, but like the other workers he enjoyed a drink after work, or in Sean's case whenever the calling beckoned, which could be anytime. Sean also possessed a very quick humour. One day about twelve men were in the process of laying many metres of concrete for the base of the new Gibraltar swimming pool, the concrete was being pumped from a line of concrete wagons standing by the side of the large base. Sean as well as helping with the concrete was overseeing the operation. As two men held and directed the large rubber pipe; which was spewing out the concrete, the other men franticly shovelled the wet concrete about the base,

Ian, one of the men spreading the concrete, required some more concrete so he shouted over to Sean.

"Hey, Sean, can you send me a little squirt over here please?"

Sean without a smile on his face looked directly at Dave, a very thin and tiny labourer and said.

"Dave, get yer self over there quick; Ian wants you."

One very hot lunch time Sean had gone to the pub, two hours later he staggered back onto the site, fortunately only minutes before John Temple appeared on the site. John possessed very little humour, but he had a quick and volatile temper, none more so than with Sean, with whom he had a love hate relationship, which Sean loved to fuel. John came rushing onto the site gripping a note book and pen in his hands, he grabbed the reading staff and the site level camera, and began opening the three-legged stilts that the camera sat on, then turning to Sean he growled.

"Sean, look through the site camera and give me a reading from these footings that's just been dug will you, I can't see the figures myself because I've left my reading glasses back at the office."

With that John walked quickly over to the other side of the site; and thrust the staff onto the bottom

of the newly dug trench. John stood impatiently looking at Sean, who in his inebriated state was swaying slightly, and trying hard to focus the camera with great difficulty. Eventually Sean bent down and peered through the back of the camera, but he quickly lifted his head back up and squinted at John. Then once again he looked back through the camera. Sean turned the knob several more times trying to focus the camera, he then shouted across to John.

"It's no good John I can't see a b------ thing, the sun is shining directly at the lens you will have to move up the trench a little bit more."

John, never patient at the best of times, was steadily building up steam, as he strode angrily further up the trench and thrust the staff violently down once more. Sean bent down again, turned the knob of the camera several more times before looking up and shouting across to John.

"It's no good John it's still dark I still can't see a b------ thing, the camera must be broke."

John gave a mighty roar and marched up angrily to Sean who was wavering unsteadily on his feet. John angrily pushed Sean out of the way, and he was just about to look through the camera himself, when he stopped, stared at the front of the camera, looked back at Sean, before he screamed at the top of his voice.

"Of course, the camera's dark, you haven't removed the f----- cover caps off the lens you stupid b-------!

Sean during the week rarely shaved in the mornings, and sometimes he would often jump straight out of bed and into his car before driving to work. One morning Phil Norton asked Sean, myself, and Mark, a labourer, to drive down to the Ocean Liner terminal building, to assess, and then engage in some work that was required. The entrance to the large pier where the ocean liners docked were strictly controlled, and a M.O.D. pass was required at all times, which most of the regular workforce possessed. Arriving at the terminal building and stepping out of the van Sean groaned softly, and held his head in his hands, looking even more hung-over than usual Sean explained that he had a very late night, and he asked would it be alright if I would look at the work to be done, while he had a quick nap. Smiling, I agreed. After I, accompanied by the labourer accessed the work we returned back to the van to go to the building merchants, but Sean was nowhere in sight. Eventually we found the bedraggled, unshaven Sean curled up fast asleep behind the terminal building. Laughing at the snoring Sean, Mark and I went to collect the materials required, knowing full well that on our return Sean would be awake and ready for work. However on our return, and after searching everywhere, Sean was nowhere to be seen. Suddenly John Temple appeared out of nowhere, and angrily demanded where we had been, but before I could reply he added.

"And just where the hell is Sean?"

At that precise moment a works van pulled up beside us, and a smiling Phil Norton; with a bemused Sean stepped out of the van, Phil then began to explain the reason behind Sean's disappearance. Apparently while Mark and I were away collecting the materials, a patrolling security officer had come upon Sean fast asleep behind the terminal building, and presuming that Sean was a trespassing tramp, he called the Gibraltar police, who quickly arrived and took the protesting Sean back to the police station. It was only after listening to Sean's explanation and phoning Phil Norton at the office to come to the police station and verify Sean's identity, that Sean was released. As Phil was explaining the story John's face grew redder and redder, and his eyes began to bulge. However, before John could exploded into one of his predictable rages, Sean simply yawned, looked at the now purple faced John and remarked innocently.

"Well I don't know about you John but I couldn't arf do with a b----- drink."

Perhaps I could recite many more characters and situations in Gibraltar that I have recalled, however like I mentioned previously that would be a book on its own. However, after that first torrid year Irena and I had settled into the Gibraltar way of life, plus we had both made a host of new friends, and we enjoyed the benefits of living in such a beautiful country. But we also had to work hard to enjoy those benefits, and although the money was not as high as in England, the weather, the new friends, and the way of life compensated in more ways than one, and yet Scarborough still remained in both of our minds.

CHAPTER 13

A BOLT FROM THE BLUE.

After serving twenty two years in the Royal Navy, Steve decided to leave the Navy and to settle in Gibraltar, so Joanna and Steve bought a three bed roomed flat in the centre of the town, and Steve started a window cleaning business, while Nicole and Jamie were settled nicely in their schools. Sharon was still single, and although Gibraltar had an influx of British armed forces, Sharon was adamant that she would never have a boyfriend in the Armed Forces, so it came as a surprise when she started dating Matt who was serving in the Royal Navy, and based in Gibraltar, and even more of a surprise when a year later Sharon announced that Matt and herself were going to get married and to hold the occasion in Gibraltar. The Wedding was a lovely happy affair, and after the service, the reception, and the evening reception were both held in the Calletta hotel that overlooked the beautiful Catlan Bay.

Irena and myself had now been working in Gibraltar for seven years, and enjoying the weather and the laid-back life style, although we did miss England at times, especially Scarborough. Never the less we had a lovely flat and we had made many friends in Gibraltar, and with Joanna and her family settling permanently in Gibraltar, and Sharon now married, it completed our happiness, although we were fully aware that Sharon and Matt, once his posting in Gibraltar was over that they would be moving back to the U.K. On a personal level I had a number of poems published in The Gibraltar Chronicle newspaper, and after successfully completing a writing course I also was now enjoying creative writing. I also wrote a few articles for the

Gibraltar Magazine. Just before we left England for Gibraltar I wrote a poem about John Lennon and it was published in a nationwide book of poems dedicated to people who had made a mark in the twentieth century. Two years later a music loving friend in Gibraltar who was a very enthusiastic Beatle fan mentioned that Yoko Ono was interested in anything positive from fans concerning her late husband, so after some persuasion from my friend although very sceptical, I sent the poem to Yoko Ono. I had completely forgotten about the poem until a few months later; when to my surprise I received from 'Studio 1'. John Lennon's recording studio in New York, a thank you card which on one side there is a dash of blue entitled 'A piece of the sky until we meet again.' with the reverse side of the card containing both John and Yoko's signatures, and although the card was one of hundreds printed it still remains a treasured possession. So it seemed that on the whole everything in my life was running smoothly, but as ever on the road of life there is always turnings, and I was now to experience a turning far beyond my comprehension.

It was the week before Christmas in 20007, Matt had been posted back to England, and with Sharon they were now living in Gosport near Portsmouth. In three weeks time I would be sixty, and although I had never bothered about my age before, it did seem like a milestone in my life. It had been a damp miserable day at work, Sean and myself, with a number of other workers had been doing repairs on a section of a brick road near the centre of the town, which we had laid in the summer months. It was very unusual for me to be ill, however I experienced what I thought was a slight chill, although I had been feeling unwell all that day. Later that afternoon Phil Norton approached Sean and myself, and gave us each a ticket for a Christmas works party that was being held that evening at a town bar, for another local building company. At first I refused the offer because I was feeling quite unwell, but when Phil, who also lived in Spain, assured me that he would be staying for only a short time himself, and I could leave my scooter at the firms yard, and he would drive me home, after some persuasion from both Phil and Sean I relented. At the party although I knew a lot of the men attending, I was still feeling unwell, and I had very little to eat or drink, however, and although not at ease I did try to join in the conversation but I was relieved when Phil announced that he was ready for home. As we crossed the border into La Linea I began to feel more unwell, and my chest started getting very tight, plus my breathing was becoming strained. Although he protested, I asked Phil to drop me off at the border on the Spanish side, to save him driving through the busy town centre. But after I stepped out of the van my chest began to get even tighter, and my head began to swoon. The walk to my flat should have only taken a few minutes, but I could only manage to walk a few breathless yards at a time before I had to stop and lean against a wall, or shop doorway, trying to catch my breath and sweating profusely. People were looking at me disapprovingly, obviously dressed in my work clothes and staggering they must have presumed that I was drunk. Eventually I did manage to reach my block of flats. However climbing the staircase to our second floor home took a great deal of effort. I vaguely remember trying to put my key into the door lock, and then the pressure on my chest became unbearable, and I stumbled onto the floor. Inside the flat Irena had heard me fumbling about with my key, but she presumed that because I had been to a party I was perhaps drunk, however she became curious; when after a few more minutes I had not entered the flat. When Irena opened the flat door she was shocked to see me lying on the landing, in pain, and gasping for breath. After quickly enlisting some help from a couple of Gibraltarian neighbours, Irena and one of the neighbours drove me to the hospital in Gibraltar. The next ten or twelve hours I can scarcely recall, but I can vaguely remember a hive of activity from the nursing staff, and an injection being put into my arm, and a mask being placed over my mouth, and being connected up to a machine, thankfully I then drifted off into a deep sleep. The next day I woke up in a very calm Intensive Care unit, feeling very disorientated. Although I tried to dismiss the thought, a doctor approached me, and after a polite detailed conversation, he confirmed that I had suffered a heart attack. It came as a surprise because for all my life I had been extremely fit and I had not suffered any illness (except for the odd flue) never mind staying in a hospital. Also, all through my working life in the building trade, apart from a few minor injuries I had always been in very good health, and my diet was well balanced, I had stopped smoking for nearly thirty five years, and I only drank moderately, so the doctors statement shocked me. After some tests I was informed that my heart was undamaged, my cholesterol was low, and my overall health for my age was excellent. The consultant undecided of the reason of my heart attack, sent me to Cadiz Hospital in Spain, for further tests. After a thorough examination the Spanish hospital found that three of my arteries had narrowed, so three stents (tiny balloons) were inflated into my affected arteries to help keep the blood flowing. A month later, feeling fit and well I returned back to work. However one tea time six weeks later, after arriving home from work, I was struggling to breathe once more, and that same tight feeling in my chest returned. Irena quickly drove me back to the Gibraltar hospital, and a second slight heart attack was confirmed. After some tests I was seen by the same consultant at the hospital who treated me for the first heart attack. He explained that two of the stents had collapsed. The consultant considered that the risk to try stents again was too great, the only alternative was to have a double heart bypass. Although the Gibraltar hospital was very modern it was not equipped for major operations, so a patient was sent to either England or Spain. My operation was to be performed in May 2007 at a newly constructed hospital called Xanit, close to Malaga on the Costa del Sol. Although I knew that my family and friends were a little apprehensive, I remained positive. The operation took three and a half hours. After I had regained consciousness, Irena and Joanna were allowed into the intensive care unit to see me. I was still very drowsy and I had wires attached all over my chest. After staying for only a few minutes Irena and Joanna decided to leave. Not long after they had departed, I began to feel very strange, and my teeth began chattering, very soon my whole body began shaking, and a bell rang above my bed, and a red light began flashing. Two nurses calmly walked over to my bed, and while one nurse fiddled with the controls on my bed head, the other nurse gave me an injection into my arm. I then drifted off into unconsciousness. When I awoke the intensive care unit was in its normal quite mode. One of the nurses appeared, and smiled, I weakly inquired what had occurred, and in broken English she explained to me that it was a normal occurrence. After being in a long operation, and the anaesthetic begins to wear off the body settles into a normal relaxed state. Later an elderly Spanish doctor in an open long white coat, and with his hands clasped behind his back, began slowly touring the ward. Seeing me awake, he came over to my bed, read my chart, and then in broken English he asked me cheerfully.

"So, Mr White, how are you?"

With wires attached to my body, and a catheter bag fastened to me, and my chest aching, I replied weakly.

"Err, not bad doctor, but I'm a bit stiff and my chest feels very sore."

The doctor stepped slightly back, and his eyes opened wide,

"Sore...sore... Yes of cause you sore Mr White you have been cut like a fish down here."

Pointing to his chest he then, in a cutting motion he drew his fingers down the full length of his own chest, while adding.

"Then three surgeons they cut your chest open, then they put their hands inside you like so."

And he demonstrated with his hands how the operation was performed. Though in pain I smiled inwardly at his brusque manner and accurate, but comical description.

After two weeks of recuperating in Hospital I was allowed home, but on strict orders to take things easy. However, I was determined not to fall into an invalid existence. Although cautious, I started doing some slight exercising and lots of steady walking, and because it was summer, a few times a week I would swim gently in the sea, in the La Linnea or the Gibraltar beaches, so generally I kept active. Nine weeks after my operation I returned back to work, feeling relaxed and strong. About four months later Irena and I were delighted when Sharon gave birth to Kirsten her first child, and our third grandchild, that news completed our happiness. A few months later Irena went back to the U.K, to visit Sharon and Kirsten for a week in October 2007 however a few days before she was due to return back from the U.K., the road of life once more produced another turning.

It was a pleasant Saturday morning, I had been tidying up the flat before Irena's expected return in a few days' time. As I walked into the lounge my left leg and arm suddenly went limp, and my head began to swoon. I slumped down onto the sofa and remained stationary as the room spun around before my eyes. After a few minutes I tried to get back up, but both my left leg and left arm were now completely lifeless, plus my head was still spinning, so I slumped back onto the sofa. I knew at once that something was amiss. I felt terribly sick but not wanting to be sick on the sofa, and with my left leg and arm lifeless I flopped down onto the floor, rolled onto on my stomach, then I managed to drag myself to the bathroom. Kneeling, and with a great deal of effort I lifted up the toilet seat and was violently sick. However, as I lifted my head up from the toilet bowl, the toilet seat suddenly dropped back down onto the top of my head, and even though I was feeling unwell I smiled inwardly at the absurd situation I had found myself in. I slowly crawled back to the lounge, and after struggling for my mobile phone, which was on the coffee table, I was able to contact Joanna (who said later that my speech was very slurred) Although it seemed like an age Joanna arrived within fifteen minutes, even though she had to cross the border from Gibraltar. Joanna went quickly to seek help from the same Gibraltarian neighbour as before, who fortunately was not at work. He went for his car and parked it right outside the building. I wasn't able to stand, because of my left arm and leg which were completely immobile, so I could not be helped to get down the hallway stairs to the car, instead I slid step by step down the staircase on my backside, and then with help from Joanna and the neighbour I managed to scramble into the car. Again I was taken to the Gibraltar hospital, (I was thinking of getting a season ticket) and after a number of questions and examinations I was removed to a side ward. The next day I was diagnosed as suffering from a slight stroke caused by a tiny blood clot in my neck. After a week's stay in the hospital, I was able to return home. My medication was revised, and after a month, I once more returned back to work.

While convalescing I had received some tragic news from Scarborough, Ted's son Paul, who was only in his early twenties, had died from an overdose of drugs. All the family knew of Paul's addiction with drugs; and of his petty thieving, but were powerless to intervene, or even to help him. Paul's death came not only as a shock to me but even more horrifying was the fact that he had died on some waste ground and it was a number of days before his body was discovered, which to me, not only was his death a terrible waste of such a young life., but that Paul, Teds son and my nephew had died alone and in terrible circumstances.

Although the rest of my body felt fine I had been getting severe back pain for some time, however I persevered and kept working until the acute pain became unbearable. Eventually I went to the doctor who diagnosed arthritis of the spine, to which he also added that any manual work was now defiantly at an end. After talking the situation over with Irena we had no option but to make an early return back to the U.K, but, there was a dilemma. For none Gibraltarians, even though you paid N. I. contributions and income tax, you are not entitled to any unemployment benefit. So, with very little money, and after most of our savings having dwindled because of my illnesses, and no sickness pay or unemployment benefits, we had only Irena's part time wages to exist, and obliviously no prospect of carrying on with my own work, so we pondered on what to do. Obliviously we would have to sell the flat to raise some money for our return, but the credit crunch had arrived, and in Spain like the rest of Europe, there was a big slump in the housing market, thus making property very hard to sell, so how would we survive financially until the flat was sold? The answer came from my friends and employers Phil and John, who suggested that they would

sack me, thus legally I would at least be able to claim unemployment benefit from Spain, of which we were residents. After a mass of paperwork, and a number of weeks back and forth to the La Linea labour exchange, I eventually began to receive generous unemployment benefit from Spain Now it seemed, that all we needed to do was to sell the flat, however our troubles were not yet over.

One morning upon awaking I clambered out of bed and fell down quickly on to the bedroom floor, with no feelings in my left leg, I knew straight away that I was experiencing another stroke and with Irena's help I once again returned to the Gibraltar hospital where it was confirmed that once more I had experienced a slight stroke. After recuperating for a few days in hospital and my medication revised once more I returned home with no after affects, except my left leg which seemed stiff I had now been unemployed for nine months, and although I received unemployment benefit from Spain, and Irena was working extra hours, we still struggled to keep our heads above water, plus my unemployment payments would gradually decrease monthly. The property market in Spain like the rest of Europe was still in a deep slump, property had been reduced drastically yet they still could not be sold. However the road of life can bring good turnings as well as bad, and in this we were fortunate. The flat had been up for sale for nearly a year with only one person showing any interest, so we were considering to lowering the price. However the next day the estate agent brought a young Spanish woman to view the flat. The woman liked what she had seen and within two months and a lot of paperwork the flat was sold. Now at last we were homeward bound.

After squaring our debts and the cost of relocating, we still had some money left over but the cost of buying a house was out of the question. At first we rented a small holiday flat in Scarborough for two weeks, while we searched for a more permanent base. However by coincidence; a few days later we met the couple who had bought the block of flats where the fire had occurred, and they themselves now occupied one of the flats, and offered to us the ground stairs flat to rent for as long as we required. Although the flat was nice Irena, thinking of myself, was dubious how I would feel after all the past turmoil, however after standing in the hallway and no flash backs; or even any feelings of foreboding I was convinced that the experience of that night had been eroded at last, and we accepted their offer. However we still wanted a permanent home, so we put our names forward to a number of social housing organisations and after eighteen months we were offered a two roomed ground floor flat belonging to one of the Social Housing company, and to my delight; only a few hundred metres from where I was born, so in reality I had completed a full circle in my life. After all the upheavals and upsets of the previous years both Irena and myself were now happy, contended, and relieved to be back home in Scarborough, and I hoped that everything was now clear ahead with no turnings, but unfortunately the road of life is never straight.

A small spot appeared behind my left ear and also an itch which irritated me, so while having a routine heart check at my local surgery the nurse prescribed for me a cream. However after two more weeks the spot had grown and the itch had turned into a pain. One month later and after a number of different prescribed antibiotics and creams my doctor referred me to Scarborough hospital, where possible skin cancer was diagnosed and a small biopsy was taken. By now the area behind my left ear was crusted and scabbed and I was in constant pain. The result of the biopsy confirmed the diagnosis, and immediately an operation was booked for me at the General Hospital in York; also because of my heart history a local anaesthetic was to be used. The operation took nearly two hours. Straight after the operation the surgeon explained that the tumour was far deeper than he had first anticipated, so he unfortunately had to remove the bottom half of my left ear, and he had also taken a biopsy of the surrounding area. The following week I was in so much pain and discomfort but I recuperated well, and two weeks later my staples and stitches were removed, and the next week I had a month of radiology therapy at Cottingham hospital. Two weeks later a small mole had now appeared on my right cheek. At Scarborough hospital a biopsy of the mole was taken for analysis, but thankfully it returned negative. So once again I looked forward to a more settled healthy life. However the pain in my back had really intensified and walking or standing for only a

few minutes was unbearable, so I was referred to a spinal consultant at Hull Royal Infirmary. A M.I. R. scan revealed that my spine was twisted and the gel in the bottom four discs of my back had eroded, also a nerve to my left leg was trapped. Three months later at the same hospital a seven operation was performed to correct these abnormities. Now, at seventy one years of age, and over six years of constant pain in my back, I am now free of pain, and I treat and enjoy each day as a new day to my life. While I was convalescing at home Joanna mentioned that she had added my name to a Face book site 'Scarborough Friends United 'at first I never bothered with it, then one day I looked on the site, and I liked the old photos of places, , and with the posts of Scarborough people and their personal reminiscences of their childhood, also a few of the people added poems that they had written, so I added a poem of my own about my younger days, and I was astounded at the response. Over the following weeks I posted a number of poems, and the likes and comments that I received were very generous and a lot of the comments suggested that I should publish a book of my poems. For a while I pondered if I should or not, one reason being I did not want a publisher to take a huge cut out of my work. Then someone recommended that I should self – publish, and also recommended a local self-publishing company 'Farthing Publishing. 'Eventually I published 60 of my poems in a book titled 'Where the Reflecting River Flows' and although I had to sell my book by myself I did recoup the money that I had paid out, and also a local Radio company 'Town and Country Radio' approached me, and now I have a spot every Monday called 'Terry's Tales'. in which I read out one of my poems.

Through these chapters I sincerely hope that I have conveyed to you the life and times of just an ordinary man, and the changes that have occurred through his lifetime. I was born just two years after the ending of the Second World War, when the mindset of Britain had altered dramatically. The generation preceding us had suffered great hardships before the war, and through that war they had witnessed much deaths, heartaches, and destruction. However, by the time I was born and although the times were still austere; and the people war weary, everything was changing for the better. That same generation demanded great changes for their future generations, for which I am personally truly grateful. My own generation have lived through decades of truly great changes in both technical and social advancement, and enjoyed much prosperity. The Building Trade in which I had spent all my working life, like so many other businesses and industries have also seen a great change, from being a labour intensified occupation to a more stream lined and technical advanced industry. Unfortunately, along with other employments the building trade has lost with that change; its characters, humour, and comradeship. Although there have been a few tragic and sad times in my life, I am grateful to have a wonderful marriage now approaching fifty years, and a truly lovely family, also in the process to have met so many people whom I can truly call my friends. However, the premature death of my nephew Paul was not only both sad and tragic, but after Irena and myself depart from this life it will also bring to an end the family name of 'White', so perhaps I am now truly at the 'End Of The Line'.

***

Printed in Great Britain
by Amazon